Routledge Library Editions

MONOPOLY AND RESTRICTIVE PRACTICES

ECONOMICS

Routledge Library Editions – Economics

INDUSTRIAL ECONOMICS
In 10 Volumes

I	Monopoly and Restrictive Practices	*Allen*
II	Effects of Mergers	*Cook*
III	Productivity and Economic Incentives	*Davison et al*
IV	An Economic Study of the City of London	*Dunning & Morgan*
V	Industry and the State	*Florence*
VI	The Logic of British and American Industry	*Florence*
VII	The Logic of Industrial Organization	*Florence*
VIII	The British Monopolies Commission	*Rowley*
IX	Studies in Industrial Organization	*Silverman*
X	Mergers and Acquisitions	*Young*

MONOPOLY AND RESTRICTIVE PRACTICES

G C ALLEN

Routledge
Taylor & Francis Group
LONDON AND NEW YORK

First published in 1968

Reprinted in 2003 by
Routledge
2 Park Square, Milton Park, Abingdon, Oxon, OX14 4RN
or
270 Madison Avenue, New York, NY 10016

First issued in paperback 2010

Routledge is an imprint of the Taylor & Francis Group

British Library Cataloguing in Publication Data
A CIP catalogue record for this book
is available from the British Library

Monopoly and Restrictive Practices
ISBN 978-0-415-31345-2 (hbk)
ISBN 978-0-415-60733-9 (pbk)
ISBN 978-0-415-31344-5 (set)

Miniset: Industrial Economics

Series: Routledge Library Editions – Economics

Monopoly and Restrictive Practices

BY

G. C. ALLEN

Emeritus Professor of Political Economy
in the University of London

Routledge
Taylor & Francis Group

LONDON AND NEW YORK

FIRST PUBLISHED IN 1968

ISBN 04 360013 I *cloth*
ISBN 04 360014 X *paper*

Preface

Monopoly and restrictive practices in some form have been with us from the beginning of modern economic society, and the law courts have long been familiar with issues raised by them. Yet, a quarter of a century ago, there would have been no point in writing a book about British experience in the control of monopoly and restrictive practices in modern times, because, except in connection with certain common law principles and their application, the author would have found little or nothing to say. Only ten years ago, an American Professor of Economics, learned in this branch of his subject, commented on the paucity of published materials on monopoly policy in the United Kingdom, in striking contrast with the huge bibliography that could be compiled for the United States.[1] Since then a remarkable change has occurred. The control of monopoly and restrictive practices has become an important constituent of British economic policy, and several valuable studies of particular aspects of the subject have lately appeared.

The present book does not aim at providing another detailed examination of the reports of the Monopolies Commission or the cases brought before the Restrictive Practices Court. Its purpose is to supply an introduction to the study of British monopoly policy by reviewing, within a framework of economic concepts, the evolution of the policy over the last twenty years. It begins with a general discussion of the monopoly problem, and then proceeds to consider particular manifestations of monopoly in modern industry. After a brief historical survey, attention is concentrated on contemporary British policy. This is the substance of the book, although room is found for a brief discussion of monopoly policy in the United States and Continental Europe. The final chapter attempts a critical appraisal of what has been achieved in the United Kingdom; it calls attention to the problems, economic and administrative, that have been encountered in the execution of the policy; and it considers the possible lines of future development.

[1] D. Dewey *Monopoly in Economics and Law*, pp. 283–4.

Restrictive practices in the labour market are beyond the scope of this book, for, although they are of outstanding practical importance, they raise problems of a special character.

The subject of monopoly and restrictive practices is one that has interested me ever since I began to study the structure of industry in this and other countries. As a temporary civil servant at the Board of Trade, during the later years of the war I was fortunate enough to be associated with the preliminary inquiries and discussions which led ultimately to the introduction of the new monopoly policy in 1948. Subsequently, for twelve years, I was a member of the Monopolies (and Restrictive Practices) Commission and had the opportunity of seeing at first hand how the policy was being administered. I should like to express my obligations to my former colleagues on the Commission; from them I learnt nearly as much as I did from the businessmen who came before us as witnesses. I thank my wife for her help in preparing the book for publication.

February 1968 G.C.A.

Contents

CHAPTER I

Monopoly and Competition in Modern Industry

At the present time the business life of this country is conducted by well over 400,000 joint stock companies, public and private, besides many unincorporated undertakings. In the manufacturing industries alone there are more than 50,000 firms employing over ten persons and a much larger number of smaller firms. The fact that for statistical and other purposes these units are classified according to industry suggests that they fall into groups with certain common interests or characteristics, and in discussions of economic policy or of the industrial structure the significance of this classification is usually taken for granted. Yet, despite these common interests and characteristics, every firm is in some way peculiar to itself, for the physical constitution and the range of its products, the conditions under which they are supplied, or its markets differ to a greater or less degree from those of others. The work done by small firms of printers or builders, or the products of members of certain manufacturing industries (e.g. woollen weaving, structural steel or pottery), bear a general resemblance to those of other firms in the same trade. But in no two firms are they precisely the same, and even the existence of a close similarity in the product itself does not necessarily accompany an identity in other respects, for example, in the markets served or in the technical conditions of production.

In some industries, notably those where close contact with customers is necessary, the sales of a typical firm are usually confined to a particular district where it may encounter very few competitors and even when a firm's business is geographically far-ranging and when it serves a national or even an international market, it is likely to conduct its affairs on the assumption that it can rely up to a point on the patronage of a solid core of customers who are not easily to be deflected to its rivals. Such confidence is the basis of its goodwill, which may constitute a most valuable asset. This quality of singularity is found among firms in industries composed of numerous members as well as those in industries dominated by one or a very few producers whose distinctive character is easily recognized. The point is then that every firm is in some sense a monopolist, the single seller of a good or service which differs in certain respects from that supplied by others.

On the other hand, it can also be asserted that all firms are competitors with one another in their efforts to meet the varied and changing demands of buyers as a whole. It is not only that shoemakers compete with shoemakers, grocers with grocers, or motor manufacturers with motor manufacturers, but also that there is some measure of competition over the whole range of goods and services supplied. We are thus confronted with what appear to be contradictory propositions, and much of the interest aroused by discussions of monopoly and competition both in academic circles and in the business world is evoked by attempts to explain or reconcile this apparent contradiction.

The problem is of some subtlety. Thus, if we start by postulating the almost universal presence of competition we must admit the qualification that all forms of competition are subject to constraints. Habits and conventions of expenditure, which may sometimes be reinforced by contracts, determine many of the decisions of purchasers over periods which may be long or short according to circumstances. These habits and conventions affect a consumer's choice of suppliers for particular types of goods and services as well as the distribution of his expenditure over broad classes of goods and services. Nevertheless, especially in a modern, dynamic society, the pattern is not immutable. Within every category of expenditure custom may be diverted from one supplier to another by the offer of goods at lower prices, by persuasive selling, or by the introduction of more acceptable varieties of goods either by established firms or by newcomers to the trade. Over the field of expenditure as a whole wants are liable to change through alterations in incomes and tastes and through the arrival in the market of new types of goods. Such innovations, as experience shows, may exert a profound effect on expenditure and so on a country's structure of production and the distribution of its manpower. Those who have witnessed the coming of the mass-produced motorcar, television and synthetic fibres do not need to be reminded of the revolutionary effects of industrial innovation on patterns of expenditure. It is true that in the short period the changes are commonly marginal—it is a question of a little more of this and a little less of that—but the cumulative influence of such changes over a decade may be conspicuous.

The changes are accompanied by the growth of some firms and the decline of others, and also by alterations in the composition of output within firms. Some firms are active in initiating the changes; others simply adapt themselves more or less successfully to shifts in demand over which they themselves exert little influence. None can hope for any long period to resist the change. Thus it follows that, even among firms which seem to dominate the market, monopoly is never for long unqualified and is always more or less vulnerable to innovations in demand and technique. So we may confidently assert that in every market monopolistic and competitive elements are present, though in widely varying proportions. At one extreme there are markets where competition reigns almost unchallenged. At the other extreme there are markets served by a single supplier. The characteristic behaviour of operators in these markets and also of those in the far more numerous markets which fall between the extremes will be considered presently.

From the standpoint of an individual firm one may imagine that its area of operations (or its markets) extends outwards in concentric circles from a fortress, which it occupies without serious challenge from its rivals, to a glacis,[1] where it enjoys a large measure of security, and then to a series of outlying zones where it meets with rivalry of increasing intensity. For some firms the proportion of trade that can be considered secure is small (in extreme cases negligible) and these firms make up the competitive sector of the economy. Others conduct the greater part of their business within the fortress or the glacis. These are the monopolists. In some cases a firm's disputed territory is under attack from numerous rivals, some of them with little secure territory of their own; in other cases, from only a few. The areas in question are not to be thought of simply as geographical areas. They are markets separated from one another by various obstacles (some geographical) which we shall later have to examine. Sometimes, as with the multi-product firm, which is typical of most large-scale or medium-scale industries, the types of goods disposed of within the fortress or glacis differ from those sold elsewhere.

The areas that fall within the various zones are not, of course, fixed over time. The glacis of a particular firm may be successfully assailed if a rival acquires new and more formidable weapons, and even its fortress may ultimately crumble. On the other hand, the trend may be in the reverse direction. An aggressive firm normally attempts to enlarge its business by establishing a supremacy in formerly disputed areas, by thrusting into places where others have hitherto enjoyed a measure of security, or by opening up new or unoccupied territories where it is for a time unchallenged. This means that it can pursue its ambitions both by introducing competition into areas where others previously possessed a monopoly, and also by enlarging the area where it can itself exert monopolistic power. On the other hand, a firm may be concerned primarily with defending its interests. It may seek to achieve this aim by devices intended to exclude rivals from disputed areas and to this extent its tactics resemble those of the aggressive firm. But it may also seek to come to an agreement with its rivals about areas

[1] The parapet which slopes from a fortress in such a way that it can be covered by fire from the ramparts.

that are to be immune from dispute, and then all parties to the agreement may turn on any outsider who tries to invade these areas.

We have shown that a firm's behaviour may vary from one of its markets to another according to the character of those markets and its own strategic aims. For the purpose of studying this behaviour more deeply, it is convenient to take two extreme cases and to consider, first, the firm which does most of its business within its fortress or glacis and, second, the firm which operates predominantly in other zones. That is to say, we shall examine the behaviour of firms in monopolistic and competitive markets respectively, and we shall ignore for the moment the strategic planning of firms, which may be concerned with the transference of activities from one type of market to another, or with changing the nature of the market itself. This behaviour has been the subject of elaborate analysis by theorists, especially those concerned with welfare economics. Their enquiries in this context have been directed chiefly to the problem of allocating resources so as to achieve the maximum satisfaction of consumers. Their reasoning has led them to the conclusion that, with a given pattern of consumer preferences, maximum efficiency is reached under conditions of perfect competition, that is to say, when the demand for the product of every firm is infinitely elastic[1] and when there is mobility of factors between industries. The conditions can be realized only where industries are composed of large numbers of firms none of dominant size, when the products of all firms are homogeneous, and when there are no barriers to the entry of firms upon new lines of production.

Having set out the conditions under which maximum efficiency in the sense defined above is to be achieved, the welfare economists then proceed to consider the effect of imperfections caused by the almost universal presence of elements of monopoly in actual market conditions. They naturally conclude that these imperfec-

[1] This means, in effect, that a firm can increase or decrease its sales without influencing the market price, which it must take as given.

tions lead to waste in the allocation of resources. Since, however, the spheres in which the conditions of perfect competition can be established or restored by legal or administrative action are few, it is commonly proposed (by those who concern themselves with policy) that a remedy be found by introducing into the world of monopoly and imperfect competition forms of behaviour equivalent to those found in the ideal world of perfect competition.

The forms of behaviour they have in mind concern primarily prices and output. Thus, in conditions of perfect competition, price is shown to be equal to marginal cost, whereas when elements of monopoly are present, price diverges from marginal cost. It should be the aim of policy (so it is argued) to secure adherence to the 'rule' that price equals marginal cost, even in situations which are far removed from perfect competition, as when the number of firms in an industry for technical and other reasons is very few. This result can be achieved either by the public operation of large-scale monopolistic enterprises (e.g. the nationalized public utilities) and by requiring the managers of such enterprises to follow the 'rule', or in private industry by the intervention of the Government to the same effect. In both cases observance of the 'rule' is likely to lead to losses by the undertakings, and the payment of subsidies by the State will thus become necessary in order that total costs shall be covered.[1]

Whatever the usefulness of this theory in enlarging our understanding of the problem of resource allocation, it is scarcely relevant to the study of the actual behaviour of monopolists and of the policies pursued by governments in regard to them. This is mainly because of the restricted meaning given by these theorists to the term 'competition', which stultifies a realistic examination of the economic situation, and partly to their neglect of some of the chief factors in economic efficiency, especially innovation and the forces

[1] In some industries the overhead costs can be recovered from consumers by a system of charging which does not affect the price of the individual units of product purchased, e.g. the two-part tariff system in electricity supply.

that promote it. The approach does not carry us far in our efforts to explain the organization of industries and the behaviour of firms in the constantly changing environment of a modern economy. Still less does it help in the framing of public policy towards that organization and behaviour.

The theoretical discussion does, however, give rise to a useful distinction with which any examination of business behaviour should start. This distinction is between the 'price-takers' and the 'price-makers', and it brings us back to the analogy of the fortress. The 'price-takers' comprise the firms whose main business is found in the disputed zones. They must accept the market price as given. Their success depends on their ability to keep their costs within the price fixed by the market and their progress turns on the amount they can profitably sell at that price. The 'price-makers', on the other hand, are firms which operate mainly in the fortress or glacis. They enjoy sufficient dominance over the market to apply their own price policy.

The distinction as set out above is too clear-cut to provide a realistic classification for all firms in the economy. First, as already shown, many firms operate in both competitive and monopolized markets. They may even sell the same class of goods in both kinds of market when these can be separated. Secondly, there are different degrees of monopoly or competition; in other words the 'mix' varies from market to market. Some markets in which a firm may appear to be a 'price-maker' may in fact be vulnerable to competition in the event of quite slight changes in costs and prices which may occur through technical or commercial innovation on the part of other firms. In such circumstances the monopolist's freedom in pricing is curtailed by his fear of potential competition. This threat is likely to be especially strong where there are on the periphery of the monopolized trade enterprising firms on the look-out for opportunities for profitable diversification, or where rapid technical changes are either altering the structure of costs or providing new means of satisfying the same wants. Again, the influence of competitive factors is likely to be strengthened in times of bad trade and weakened in booms. In persistently inflationary conditions it may progressively decline over a wide range of industries, just as a firm which is experiencing a rapid expansion of demand for its products will be relieved of competitive pressures. Legal and institutional changes may also exert an effect. For instance, alterations in tariffs or other protective devices and in the patent law may either enlarge or contract the area of competition. Similar results will attend technical changes which either increase or diminish the optimum size of the units of production, and so the number of firms, in an industry.

The discussion so far has not provided us with an answer to the important practical question of how monopoly and competition respectively affect economic welfare. We have already referred (see page 15 *supra*) to the argument that monopoly is a source of waste and inefficiency because it distorts the allocation of productive resources (capital, labour and natural resources). In other words, by driving these resources into uses different from those to which they would be put if conditions of perfect competition prevailed, it is likely to reduce the value of the national output. Monopoly also, so it is contended, brings about a biased distribution of the national income. This occurs because a monopolist's control over the prices of his products enables him to earn abnormal profits at the expense of firms in the competitive sector and of consumers as a whole. But these conclusions rest on the assumption of the ideality of perfect competition, and they neglect the question of the relative technical and commercial efficiency of monopolistic and competitive undertakings, especially the contribution of each type to innovation and economic progress. Since most of the advances in real income have been achieved by the successful application of scientific invention and by improvements in productive and marketing organization, judgment must turn on relative capacities in these respects rather than on allocative effects. It is true that the latter, which have to do with the distribution of the national income as well as the use of resources, cannot be ignored in any discussion of monopoly and competition. Yet, in any analysis of this problem, attention should be directed mainly towards the dynamic aspect, at any rate if material progress is accepted as the leading purpose of economic policy.

It may be useful at this point to summarize the conclusions so far reached. The outstanding feature of a monopoly is that the seller has the power to fix the terms on which buyers must take his goods, and ultimately his power rests on the fact that no close substitutes for his product are available. Competition in its perfect form exists where the demand for the products of an individual firm is infinitely elastic, for in such circumstances it cannot raise its net revenue by withholding supplies from sale and it must take the market price as given. These are formal descriptions of limiting cases. Most situations in the real world combine elements of both monopoly and competition, and for particular producers or industries the combination is constantly being modified under the influence of technical advances and changing demands. Monopoly is liable to be eroded by the appearance of substitutes for the monopolized product or by the incursion of newcomers into the monopolized field. And the threat to established positions, that is, the existence of potential competition, limits in varying degrees the freedom of the monopolist in using his powers. On the other hand, even in industries composed of numerous rival firms, competition is usually imperfect, at any rate for part of their sales. The imperfection may arise simply through the existence of goodwill created by previous business operations, or through differences in location and the incidence of transport costs, or through product differentiation which may be accidental or deliberate. Here again, the position in most industries is unlikely to be stable for very long, since the extent or vigour of competition may well be affected by the cheapening of transport, the reduction of import duties, the removal of legal or institutional barriers to competition, the standardization of goods hitherto produced in variety, or the reverse of any of these changes.

It might be supposed that, in a world of dynamic economies, all monopolies would be insecure for the reasons already discussed.

But this conclusion, though it is probably true in the long run and for large sectors of industry, cannot be accepted without qualification, for the strength of monopolists may be fortified in various ways. These may become clear if we consider some of the routes by which monopoly may be achieved. First, independent firms may be merged financially and the new organization so created may become responsible for a high proportion of a product and related products. Alternatively, a firm may grow disproportionately to others in the same trade so that it achieves dominance. In some cases its growth may result from its superior efficiency, in other cases from its use of devices which exclude competitors from its markets. Then, the State may confer privileges on a producer, as by the grant of patent rights. Finally, a number of independent firms may enter into restrictive arrangements with one another and these may not merely destroy or diminish competition with each other, but may also leave little opportunity for outsiders. A particular firm may achieve monopoly by the use of several of these routes.

Even where numerous independent firms continue to serve the market without collusion, competition may nevertheless be restrained. In some industries each firm may take deliberate measures to create zones of security for itself by product differentiation, that is to say, by branding its goods and building up goodwill for its brands by advertisement and other forms of 'merchandising'. In other industries, despite the existence of several independent firms, one producer, because of its size or its strategic advantages in the market, may be accepted as the price leader for certain products, and the rest may find it expedient to follow any changes in price which it chooses to make. This practice may come into existence without collusion or agreement, because both the leader and the followers are anxious to avoid price competition which would have adverse effects on profits. Where the number of producers in an industry is small, unrestrained price competition may well be very dangerous and the outcome uncertain. In such circumstances every firm, before it makes any price change, is likely to consider the probable effects on the price policy of the others, for if its action should lead to a price war, all the firms might suffer. This is a situation characteristic of oligopoly which is found over a wide range of modern industry.

The importance of these restraints on competition differ widely from one trade to another, even among those that are structurally similar, and it may easily be exaggerated. Even where firms avoid the kind of price competition liable to produce retaliation they often seek to improve their position in the industry by other means. They may introduce new varieties of the product and offer these at lower prices. They may adopt methods of competition other than price competition. These include competition in service, advertising or selling effort. These forms of competition are generally regarded by welfare economists as less socially beneficial than price competition because whereas the latter is calculated to lower prices, the alternative method will almost certainly result in a rise of selling costs. A final judgment, however, must depend on the ultimate effect of the behaviour on the whole cost and price structure of the firms.

Whatever the methods of competition adopted by oligopolists, it is unlikely that shares in the market will remain unchanged for very long. This will apply even to firms that collude with one another in regard to prices and market quotas. The firms which are openly or tacitly adhering to a common price structure are unlikely to have identical levels of costs. The low-cost firms will consequently make higher profits, and these will enable them to extend their marketing efforts or to invest in new processes or in other innovations which may ultimately enable them to cut their prices without fear of retaliation. Firms unable to adopt similar measures will lose ground. Thus, competition among oligopolists and members of cartels is by no means unknown, even though it manifests itself in different ways from those found in the obviously more competitive industries. Oligopoly, or even cartelization, does not necessarily imply stagnation (or stability).

The degree of competition in oligopolistic situations varies widely according to the cost structure of the several firms and the character of the management. An industry under the control of alert and aggressive policy makers will provide plenty of examples of inter-firm rivalry even if it is composed of very few firms. On the other hand, a multi-firm industry which superficially appears to offer ample opportunities for competition of the classical type may in fact be much less vigorously competitive if it is in the hands of routineers or managers content with a quiet life. Experience certainly does not suggest that all the most progressive industries are those which most nearly satisfy the conditions of perfect competition.

CHAPTER II

Workable Competition and Effective Business Performance

The argument in the previous chapter points to the conclusion that, in order to reach an understanding of the industrial structure and behaviour that promote economy, efficiency and progress (and also of the criteria that should govern policy towards monopoly), we need a definition of competition more useful than that provided by welfare theory. Such a definition was offered by Professor J. M. Clark in his paper on 'Workable Competition'.[1] The theory of workable competition is concerned with the factors that stimulate economic rivalry and is, therefore, a dynamic concept. It tries to judge forms of industrial organization and the policies of firms by reference to the extent to which they promote or hamper this rivalry. It recognizes that monopoly elements are inevitably present in most market situations in modern industry and it seeks the ways in which these can be made compatible with active competitive behaviour. The main condition for the existence of workable competition is that both buyers and sellers should have before them 'an adequate number of alternative courses of action'. This concept is far from precise, and leaves the determination of what is 'adequate' to be decided in particular cases. Further, one must recognize that the existence of opportunities for competition does not ensure that they will be seized. This depends on the presence of a desire for active behaviour, or of an aggressive spirit, somewhere in the industry.

[1] 'Towards a Concept of Workable Competition', in *American Economic Review*, June 1940.

So, workable competition, according to this argument, describes the kind of market pressure which must be exerted to penalize laggards and to reward the enterprising, and in this way to promote economic progress. Clearly, such pressures are not found in all markets to an equal extent. Where a market is served by a single firm, or by firms bound by restrictive contracts, the conditions are obviously not present, especially if the trade is one which is difficult for newcomers to enter. It is true that, as already shown, competitive pressures can seldom be wholly abolished and that in the long run they are likely to appear in almost every market. Yet, for a considerable period and over a wide area of an economy they may be impeded. Where alert entrepreneurship is scarce and technical innovation slow, a positive policy designed to remove hindrances to workable competition may be necessary for progress. In all societies, indeed, there are likely to be dormant areas which, unless roused by attack from some authority charged with the control of monopoly, will remain a burden on the economy.

Workable competition, therefore, remains as a general condition of economic efficiency and progress and as a handy tool of policy. But it cannot be left in triumphant possession of the whole field. For in judging any economic situation we must have regard not merely to market conditions but also to the actual measured performance of different types of firms. Now when we consider performance, the devastating attack by Professor Schumpeter on the conventional attitude of the economist towards monopoly cannot be ignored. Schumpeter holds that the common view of monopoly as a structure damaging to the public interest is entirely unjustified. According to him the ordinary forms of price competition favoured by economists and anti-trust bodies can at best only protect consumers against being charged excessive prices in relation to current levels of cost. But the competition which counts is not that among firms with broadly similar techniques and forms of organization, but competition from new commodities and new technology, new sources of supply and new types of organization. This latter type of competition, which owes its origin to progressive technique and organization is fundamental, for it alters the whole cost structure of industry. Furthermore, the changes in demand which often affect established positions in industry are themselves the result of the initiative of firms in devising new products and in marketing them. In other words, what is most significant for economic progress is a process of 'creative destruction', the overwhelming of established producers and methods of production by innovation.[1]

This proposition undoubtedly provides a key to economic progress in modern industrial societies, but it is only the starting point of the argument. Schumpeter then goes on to assert that monopoly is highly conducive to, indeed is a condition of, the continuing process of innovation. He bases his assertion on the proposition that only very large organizations, which are protected from the full impact of competition, are able to lay their hands on the resources which permit them to bring innovations to fruition as well as to meet the risks of introducing them. Without the high profits which their monopoly enables these concerns to earn, both the incentive and the means to innovate would be lacking. It follows that efforts to destroy monopoly by legislative or administrative action are misguided. These views of the beneficence of monopoly and oligopoly as instruments of technical and economic change are in line with those of several other American economists.

The arguments have force. It can be conceded that large-scale industry is associated with a high rate of technical progress and that high profits are necessary if firms are to meet the risks of massive investment in new techniques. But we must make reservations. First, it is not true that all innovations have flowed from the great firms. Some of the outstanding pioneers in recent times have been found among small and medium-sized firms. What is more, many important innovations have been introduced by such firms in the face of the scepticism of the large firms. Established producers have often greeted inventions with distaste or indifference and have only taken them up when others have shown their worth.

[1] J. A. Schumpeter, *Capitalism, Socialism and Democracy*, p. 84.

Professor Jewkes and his colleagues have provided impressive lists of inventions and of market innovations in which the lead has been taken by small firms. This is not to deny that very large-scale organization is inevitable in many of the science-based industries, nor that great firms have often played an essential part in the development stage between the invention and the market innovation. But it would be imprudent for a country to become dependent solely on a few large organizations for contributions to its economic progress, for by no means all great firms are alert and enterprising. Furthermore, Schumpeter's insistence on the role of 'creative destruction' in progress suggests that he is not defending monopoly as such but rather that he is concerned with enlarging the concept of competition. It is not the great monopoly with its market power and capacity for earning high profits that he defends, but only such of them as make use of their power to innovate and to compete effectively with conservative routineers. Indeed, the competitive power which a great firm possesses, or which it fears may be exerted against its own interests by other innovators, is of utmost significance in maintaining a high rate of progress in a modern economy. During the present century the barriers between once separate industries have been breaking down. Great firms have been extending their empires by 'muscling into' trades previously regarded as the province of others. A monopolistic position achieved by a firm in one field is seldom immune for very long from attack by other firms previously associated with quite different industries.

There are, however, contrasts between various parts of the industrial field. There are some industries where the dominant firms are frequently exposed to this type of attack. There are others where a monopolist has little to fear from potential competition. Judgment about the danger of monopolistic structures to the public interest must, therefore, vary according to these circumstances. 'Atomistic' competition in industries in which technical

[1] J. Jewkes, D. Sawers and R. Stillerman, *The Sources of Invention*, *passim*.

economies can be reached only in very large plants is impossible. But this is not to deny that some sort of competitive pressure, including the potential competition of great firms in other industries, is necessary in order to ensure that a dominant firm is kept up to the mark. So, competition which Schumpeter expelled by one door returns by another. Although one must admit that, without applying the test of performance, it would be rash to assert that the infusion of more competition into a particular monopolized industry would *necessarily* increase its efficiency, it is also clear that where workable competition is absent (that is, where there are no alternative choices for customers or suppliers) performance tests are difficult to apply.[1]

A realistic discussion of the monopoly problem is complicated by the fact that businessmen, in seeking to justify the creation of monopolistic organization, seldom draw the distinction (which seems fundamental to economists) between developments that are necessary to realize the economies of scale and those that are designed to increase market power. The confusion is understandable. A combination which extinguishes the competition hitherto present among independent firms may promote productive economies at the same time as it enhances the market power of the combined producers. Those whose concern is primarily with increasing profitability can see no point in drawing a distinction which for them can have no practical importance. One must add that it is extremely difficult after a lapse of time for an outsider (or even for a member of an industry) to discover which motive predominated when the combination was formed, and whether the degree of monopoly achieved was greater than was necessary to permit the realization of the economies of scale.

[1] Tests of performance frequently suggested include: (*a*) progressiveness, especially in regard to a firm's record in innovation; (*b*) a satisfactory price policy, with particular reference to the firm's practice in passing on or not passing on reductions in costs to customers in the form of lower prices; (*c*) appropriate size of investment in relation to the output; (*d*) a reasonable level of profits in comparison with firms in related branches of industry.

The point is very relevant to any examination of mergers. Most dominant firms in industries where economies of scale are decisive have reached their position both by internal growth and by mergers. The relative importance of the two processes in particular cases have depended largely upon how far competition has been effective, in the period before the merger, in eliminating high-cost producers and so achieving a 'higher organization'. In some industries its effectiveness may have been reduced by agreements for market-sharing, in others by product-differentiation which may have been supported by 'stand-off' sales efforts (that is, marketing devices introduced by a particular firm simply because its rivals have introduced them). Or the effectiveness of competition may have been weakened by a reduction in the number of firms before any of them had reached the optimum size.[1] In all these cases, rationalization, that is, consolidation in the industry designed to provide access to the full economies of scale, might be expected to eliminate waste and reduce costs. If this aim is achieved, the consolidation will have been justified by its performance. But whether it will continue to be progressive may well depend subsequently on surviving market pressures exerted by potential competitors on the periphery of the industry.

Where the merger has been undertaken solely or mainly to increase the market power of the firms, and if the productive economies that are incidentally realized are small, its advantages from the standpoint of efficiency and the public interest are likely to be insignificant or even negative. Such mergers, however, do not usually survive very long. Investigations into a number of British mergers led to the conclusion that mergers were seldom successful in the long run unless they yielded economies of scale.[2] In other words, in the absence of such economies, competitive pressures were sufficient ultimately to erode the market power initially achieved. However, the qualification 'ultimately' is impor-

[1] Cf. D. Dewey, 'Mergers and Cartels: Some Reservations About Policy', in *American Economic Review*, May 1961, pp. 258–9.

[2] P. Lesley Cook and Ruth Cohen, *Effects of Mergers*, p. 442.

tant, for the progress of an economy may for a time be hampered by mergers of that kind.

In general, economic opinion has been more favourably disposed towards close combines (monopolies of scale)[1] than towards cartels which are associations of financially independent traders. This is because the main function of cartels is to curtail competition by such devices as minimum price agreements, output or sales restrictions, market sharing, and exclusive dealing arrangements between manufacturers and distributors which block the access of outsiders to the market. It is not obvious that cartels can bring economies of production to offset the disadvantages to consumers of these devices, whereas monopolies of scale (close combines) at any rate provide the opportunities of achieving such economies. It is partly for this reason that anti-monopoly policy in modern times has mounted a more vigorous attack on cartels than on monopolies of scale.[2]

There is no reason to reject this distinction, but something can be said on the other side. Some cartels, as well as some mergers, are aimed at the elimination of waste. For instance, cartels that provide for the sharing of technical knowledge and the inter-licensing of patents may reduce the cost of research and development and may stimulate technical advance in the group of firms covered by the agreement. Of course, if the arrangement is accompanied by restrictions on the licensing of patents to outsiders, the general economic advantage is likely to be reduced. Furthermore, it is sometimes contended that technical progress is more rapid if competition extends to research as well as to production and marketing; this argument is difficult either to prove or to disprove. Some cartels, notably those concerned with agricultural raw materials subject to violent cyclical fluctuations, are aimed at

[1] The term 'monopoly of scale' is widely used in Great Britain nowadays to describe a single-firm monopoly or close combine.

[2] This is not the only reason. Those responsible for the execution of the policy find it easier to identify the disadvantages of cartels and to find evidence about them than they do in regard to monopolies of scale (see Chapter IX).

maintaining price stability, which is usually beneficial to producers and consumers alike. Unfortunately, whatever may be said in principle in favour of such cartels, their experience has been unfavourable. Some have succeeded in holding prices steady for a time only to collapse ultimately with disastrous results for the organized producers. Their failure can usually be attributed to their inability to distinguish cyclical fluctuations from secular trends. This confusion has disposed them to maintain prices at a level consistently higher than that which equated long-run supply and demand, with the result that new sources of supply have been drawn in and excessive stocks accumulated. On grounds of performance, therefore, the scales are weighted against cartels when they are compared with monopolies of scale. On the other hand, from the standpoint of workable competition the balance of advantage is reversed. Cartels are terminable associations and their members retain their separate existence. While they may damp down competition, their attempts to eliminate it are seldom completely successful. If their members are precluded from competing on price, they can do so in other ways, and frequent adjustments in the arrangements are necessary to accommodate the restrictions to changes in the relative strengths of firms.

So far we have confined our attention to the private sector. In all modern economies, however, the State intervenes in the conduct of industry, and the use of its power in creating or buttressing monopoly cannot be ignored. Public monopolies have been created in several industries, as in the British nationalized industries run either by Government departments (e.g. the Post Office) or by publicly appointed boards (e.g. the National Coal Board). Within most of the industries which have been nationalized the scope of the monopoly is all-embracing and its authority unchallengable. But even here the market power of a public monopoly may be qualified by the presence of substitutes provided by other industries. For example, the nationalized coal industry competes in the fuel and power market with several other nationalized power industries and also with the privately owned oil and natural gas industries. The nationalized railway industry is confronted by privately owned road operators and shipping lines in some branches of its business.

The State has also created or supported monopolistic organization in a number of private industries. During the decade before the Second World War, the Government actively encouraged the cartelization of British industry and it even compelled the coal-mining industry by legislation to introduce restrictive practices.[1] The various agricultural marketing boards fall into the same category. These State-supported or operated cartels have been among the most powerful and durable in the country. Several international cartels have also been set up by a number of governments acting in concert, e.g. the International Wheat Agreement and the International Sugar Council.

The importance of public monopoly and of State-supported cartels has grown conspicuously during the last few decades. The nationalized industries themselves now employ over 10 per cent of Britain's total occupied manpower. This is a sector where organization is rigid. At first sight there seems a strange inconsistency in the Government's action in extending State monopoly at a time when it had begun to attack private monopoly. To a considerable extent, however, the nationalized sector is composed of those industries in which opportunities for competition are necessarily limited. This applies especially to the 'natural' monopolies, the public utilities. These usually require the use of the public domain which cannot be granted unreservedly, and they operate with capital installations the size of which is determined by the extent of the market allotted to them by edict or administrative action. They include electricity supply, gas supply, urban transport and the mainline railway system. Even in the days when these industries were privately run, the charges made by them were subject to public control in order to protect the users from exploitation. In these industries competition is not a real alternative to monopoly, and ownership (and operation) by the State or its agents is one

[1] This policy is considered further in Chapter III.

among several methods of safeguarding customers against the abuses of private monopoly. It may sometimes also provide the most economical means of operation. In other industries, e.g. agriculture, State-operated or supported cartels are designed to promote political, strategic or social policies which have been decided on for reasons which have little to do with economic efficiency. Public monopoly, therefore, is a special case. Although it forms an important field of economic enquiry, it must be discussed in a rather different context from that of private monopoly with which this book is concerned.

These references to public monopoly, however, have brought into the open certain considerations which have been implicit in our discussion of private monopoly. The analysis of forms of economic organization or policy in this field rests on certain assumptions about economic and social purposes. In other words, they proceed from 'value judgments' which economic theory must take as given and for which it is not itself responsible. The discussion so far has been conducted on the assumption that a leading aim of policy is to promote not only efficiency (in the sense of the ideal allocation of resources), but also economic growth, that is, a constant enlargement of output and income. Progress is considered to be more important than stability. This implies that it is more desirable that output and income should grow fast than that firms or individuals should be protected against economic change or that established relations should continue unaltered. Societies have existed to which change was repugnant, and in them policy was directed towards maintaining the status quo.[1] They viewed the competitive system with distaste, and their sentiment cannot be refuted by economic reasoning. Most contemporary societies, however, are intent upon maintaining a high rate of economic progress and their general view of monopoly and restrictive practices should be consistent with this aim. It may perhaps be questioned whether in modern times the dichotomy between

[1] For example, Imperial China in the century or more before the Revolution of 1911.

stability and progress is really as sharp as it appears, for a policy of resisting change is probably incompatible today with the maintenance of stability. This argument, however, need not be pursued. The point for emphasis is that our conclusions about monopoly and restrictive practices, and about policies towards them, are based on the proposition that economic growth is among the leading purposes of a modern society.

In popular discussion, attitudes to monopoly and restrictive practices have been much influenced by the belief that monopolies exploit consumers, in the sense that they benefit the profit earners (and wage earners employed by the monopolies) at the expense of the rest of the community. Even if the replacement of competition in industry by a monopoly of scale sometimes reduces the costs of production, it is widely held that these benefits are not passed on to consumers. Furthermore, there is, in some countries more than in others, a strong sentiment in favour of the 'small man' and keen public sympathy for him in his struggle with great firms. When this sentiment is reflected in policy, in circumstances in which the great firms enjoy superior efficiency, then the effect may be to retard a shift in production to low-cost suppliers. This is sometimes a source of inconsistency in monopoly policy, as we shall see.[1] Finally, it may be considered desirable for the political health of a nation that the concentration of economic power should be discouraged and numerous points of independent initiative sustained. This preference is often supported by arguments of another character. Thus it is possible to admit that in certain industries a high concentration of control may result in the short run in lower costs of production than would dispersion, and yet to contend that for the preservation of a lively innovating spirit a competitive structure which provides opportunities for experiment with alternatives is to be preferred to a monolith. Here we encounter a conflict between short-run and long-run advantages, which cannot be solved within a narrow economic context.

[1] See, especially, Chapter X below.

CHAPTER III

Cartels, Combines and Industrial Concentration

The routes to monopoly are very numerous and it would be tedious to attempt to provide anything approaching a complete list of them. We cannot proceed further with our study, however, until the most commonly used have been described. We have already referred to the broad distinction between terminable associations and close combines (or monopolies of scale), that is to say, between monopolies that rest upon restrictive agreements for a term of years among independent firms, and those which depend upon the dominance of single firms and in which the separate identities of former members of the industry have been wholly or largely destroyed by financial combination. At the extremes this distinction is sharp, but there is a wide area where it becomes blurred and imprecise. This, indeed, is true of almost every kind of industrial classification.

In the first group a detailed classification must depend partly on the form of the agreements and partly on their content. Terminable associations range from informal tacit understandings to elaborate organizations that rest upon written agreements and are served by central secretariats appointed by the constituent firms. The informal understandings, often known as 'gentlemen's agreements', are numerous. Many of them are found among firms serving particular localities (e.g. local firms of bakers or brick-makers), but in industries where the number of independent firms is few they may have a nation-wide coverage. This type of agreement may be concerned with minimum prices, common discounts, areas to be served, or channels of sale. The understandings are not embodied in any written contract. Indeed, they may not even require an explicit understanding or undertaking on the part of firms to observe any common rules. As in the famous Gary Dinners, attended by members of the United States steel industry in the early years of this century, prices may be merely mentioned and no one may be required to commit himself to an agreed course of action.[1] But the expectation is that the prices mentioned will become the common prices charged by all members of the trade.

In some industries the meetings of representatives of the different firms may provide the means by which the firm accepted as a price leader communicates its intentions to the rest. Here also there is no need for even verbal commitments. For example, price leadership in the British motor tyre industry during the nineteen-fifties was facilitated by periodical informal meetings among the firms, and in evidence to the Monopolies Commission the participants denied that they went further than the exchange of information and the discussion of prices. In such instances it may well be that no further action is necessary in order to achieve the desired result. Where the law is hostile to cartels, informal arrangements are often preferred by the business world because the collusion is more difficult to prove. The price associations in the British timber import trade, after their formal cartel had been condemned by the Monopolies Commission and the Government, were able for a time to preserve what they called 'the structure of prices' simply through indirect pressure exerted on those who were disposed to disregard that structure. In favourable conditions, when the industry is composed of very few firms with strong common interests, these informal understandings may be extremely powerful.

They are unlikely to be successful, however, where there are numerous firms in an industry and where, because of the nature of the product or the market, price lists are elaborate and complicated.

[1] The Gary Dinners were held periodically at the house of Judge Gary, the Chairman of the United States Steel Corporation, and were attended by the chief magnates in the steel industry.

In such industries the pursuit of monopoly will depend on a formal contract which sets out an agreed list of prices and rules of trading. In the calico printing industry, for example, where the number of separate items of work done is enormous, the agreed price list was a lengthy document. A shipping conference, which often covers all the cargo liners sailing between specified ports, will likewise have written agreements about freight rates for different types of goods and also the terms of deferred rebates to be paid to loyal shippers. Some of the formal cartels operate with a secretariat responsible to the member firms. For instance, the secretariat of the Motor Trade Association issued information to its members concerning the list prices of new cars, trading-in prices and other conditions. Some associations impose sanctions against those who break the rules, e.g. price cutters of goods subject to resale price maintenance. The question of sanctions will be considered further presently.

Many cartels are not content to limit their restrictive activities to prices. This is for two reasons. First, they are often obliged to take action to strengthen the market position of the associated firms against outsiders and to discourage any potential new competitors. Secondly, they may find it necessary to reinforce the loyalty of members to the rules. So, minimum price agreements are often buttressed by exclusive dealing arrangements between manufacturers and distributors which seek to deny to would-be competitors access to the market. If a cartel manages to include a high proportion of the most important distributors within such arrangements, the path of a newcomer may be effectively blocked. Sometimes the agreement provides for sharing of the markets. Or control may be imposed over the output or the sales of members. In some industries (e.g. cotton spinning) this policy has been carried out by restricting the proportion of the machines to be operated in each factory or the number of working days per week. Alternatively, every firm may be allotted a share or quota of the total sales. If it should exceed its quota, it is fined; if it falls short it is compensated. Such an arrangement, even if not combined with the setting of an absolute limit on the quantity of sales, is calculated to discourage competition among the members by reducing the profit to be earned on any excess above the quota. Although the more progressive firms may constantly exceed their quota and be content to pay the fines because of the cost advantages of 'running full', nevertheless, the retarding effect is still present. Quotas seldom remain unchanged for long periods. Firms that normally exceed their quotas will press for an increase whenever the agreement comes up for review, and the stability of the cartel may be threatened if these claims are resisted. The rules of some cartels provide for automatic increases or decreases in quotas by reference to past performance.

Competition for quotas may be a source of weakness in cartels, and where it is keen there is reason for supposing that the common interests of the firms are weak and rivalries intense. The problem of maintaining loyalty in these circumstances may tax the ingenuity of those in charge of policy. From the standpoint of a particular producer, an ideal condition exists if he finds a means of breaking the rules himself while other members of the trade adhere to them. With this in mind, firms sometimes try to defeat the common pricing rules by offering customers secret rebates, by supplying goods of a higher quality than those invoiced, by establishing trading subsidiaries whose connections with the parent concerns are not known to outsiders, or even by integrating with customers. The cartels try to combat these 'disloyal' practices by introducing rules about credit terms, discounts and delivery terms. They regulate the quality or specifications of the goods in order to facilitate control over prices and the volume of sales. They seek to sustain the quota system by providing for the transference of quotas among members on terms to be fixed by the association. The developing firm may thus be able to work near to capacity, while the seller of the quota may be satisfied with an income earned by refraining from production. There have been cases in which the sellers of quotas have closed down altogether.

The cartels sometimes impose penalties for breaches of the rules. Yet, where the firms in an industry are producing at very different levels of cost, it is not easy to assure the loyalty of all members. In bad times, in particular, the temptation to snatch a selfish advantage may be irresistible to a firm without ample financial resources. In conditions of this kind those responsible for the administration of cartels are inclined to be cautious in their price policy. Thus, the power of cartels, and so their economic effects, vary widely from one to another according to the character of the membership and the state of the market. In the deflationary conditions of the nineteen-thirties the capacity of private cartels to restrain competition was narrowly limited, but this did not prevent an increasing elaboration in their rules.

It quite often happens that the restrictive arrangements introduced by cartels tend to become more complicated than effective. When a secretariat is set up, the chief officers may develop a strong professional interest in enhancing the power of the cartel. If they are energetic and ingenious, they may exert themselves to persuade their members to agree to a proliferation of the restrictions. There have been instances in which the principals of the associated firms have found themselves committed to restrictions far more elaborate than they themselves had intended to introduce. This may be regarded as an example of Parkinson's Law operating in a specialized bureaucratic field.[1]

In industries where orders are allotted after tender, as in the building industry, the shipbuilding industry or some branches of engineering, the associations have found other ways of restricting competition. Their rules may provide for joint consultation before tendering. The procedure laid down is usually designed to ensure for each firm a 'fair' share of contracts over a period or to avoid

[1] The machinery for administering quota arrangements, especially by large international cartels, is sometimes very elaborate. The Monopolies Commission reported in 1951 that the Administrative Office set up to deal with the returns of the electric lamp manufacturers under the Lamp Agreement of 1948, had to analyse about 200,000 invoices a month. This, it was noted, was equivalent to two-fifths of the number of customs documents handled monthly for producing the Trade and Navigation Returns of the United Kingdom. See *Report on the Supply of Electric Lamps*, p. 38n.

unprofitable tenders. Payments are usually made by those who receive the contract to those who refrain from tendering or who deliberately tender high. In the London building industry, for example, an elaborate system was devised for maintaining a profitable level of prices. It will be described in Chapter VI.

Some cartels provide for arrangements between manufacturers on the one hand and the suppliers of machinery or materials on the other. These arrangements try to ensure that supplies are withheld from outsiders, or are supplied to them on more onerous terms than to the members. The British and Swedish match manufacturers, for instance, had an agreement of this sort in regard to the supply of match-making machinery to 'outsiders'.[1] A variety of this type of restriction once existed in the boot and shoe trade. The United Shoe Machinery Company, which had a monopoly of many kinds of machinery, leased the plant to boot and shoe manufacturers on condition that the latter refrained from using certain kinds of machinery available from other suppliers.[2] Sometimes the intention is to exert monopsonistic power over the suppliers. Thus, the steel makers' cartels have long had arrangements for the joint purchase of scrap which is subsequently distributed among their members. Finally, there are the arrangements between manufacturers and distributors (wholesalers or retailers) for the maintenance of fixed or minimum resale prices. This practice will receive detailed attention later on. Exclusive dealing arrangements between manufacturers and distributors also fall into this general category.

The cartel reaches another stage when it makes provision for the joint selling of the products of the associated manufacturers. Where this is done, the individual manufacturers may give up their own selling organization and a joint selling agency or syndicate may handle the whole of the business, allotting sales to the different

[1] See Monopolies and Restrictive Practices Commission, *Report on the Supply and Export of Matches and the Supply of Match-Making Machinery*, pp. 35, 88.

[2] Board of Trade Working Party Report, *Boots and Shoes*, p. 15.

participants in agreed proportions. For instance, up to a few years ago the Sulphate of Ammonia Federation controlled the sales of ammonium sulphate produced both by the great chemical firms, which used a synthetic process, and also by the gas works and coke producers as a by-product. Imperial Chemical Industries acted as the central sales agent for the whole supply.[1]

We have already observed that cartels are frequently troubled by the problem of maintaining loyalty, since the interests of the various members seldom coincide for long. The fines for over-selling, as described above, should not be regarded wholly as a penalty for actions contrary to the cartel rules, since they, like the compensation for under-selling, are often seen as balancing factors in the restrictive agreement as a whole. The primary object of 'loyalty rebates' or 'loyalty discounts' on selling prices is, however, that of tying distributors or users to the associated manufacturers. The more elaborate cartels have introduced many devices for enforcing their rules. Some of them in the past established a quasi-judicial procedure for dealing with distributors suspected of cutting maintained prices. Their private courts were able to bring strong pressure on those whose offences were proved. If warnings were ineffective, then the offender might be boycotted, that is to say, the associated manufacturers would be forbidden to supply him. Some cartels have been accustomed to levy their members to provide funds for subsidising sales in markets threatened by outsiders. Money raised in this way has been used to buy off competition, as when payments are made to firms on condition that they give up their plans for extending production.

Cartels which derive their strength from privileges conferred by the State are normally in a far stronger position than others. In recent decades some of the most powerful cartels have been promoted or buttressed by legislation. Examples are to be found in the associations of producers established by the Coal Mines Act of 1930 for fixing prices and restricting output, and in the Agricultural

[1] Monopolies Commission, *Report on the Supply of Chemical Fertilisers*, pp. 27–8.

Marketing Boards set up shortly afterwards for controlling certain agricultural products. Again, the Cotton Industry Reorganization Act of 1939 gave the associations of cotton spinners authority to fix minimum prices under certain conditions, although the outbreak of the war prevented this Act from coming into force. Arrangements for restricting competition have also been introduced by the Government into the fishing industry, inland transport and several other trades. State-supported cartels, it may be contended, are scarcely in pari materia with purely private cartels, for it is to be presumed that the former are concerned with carrying out national policies which may be determined by other than economic considerations. Such policies, although they are quite properly the subject of criticism, lie outside the scope of a book of this kind. But two aspects of this type of cartel can be considered to fall within our province. First, we may ask whether the means employed are the most economical that can be devised for achieving the aims of the Government. Secondly, we must note that such cartels are likely to be far more stable than those without legislative support. This point is of significance in any survey of the part played by competitive forces in the economy as a whole.

The State also affects the form of cartels through the grant of patent rights. These are intended to encourage invention by giving inventors and those who develop their inventions a safeguard against the risks of competition. The relevance of this principle to the arguments of Schumpeter, as set out in the previous chapter, should not be overlooked. Our immediate concern with patents, however, is derived from the fact that they sometimes form the basis of restrictive agreements which go far beyond the temporary quasi-monopoly conferred by the grant of the patent. A simple agreement by the patent holder to license a user does not, of course, have any such restrictive effect. But some patent agreements are drawn so as to limit the rights of the parties in using the patents or in licensing them. They may provide for the grant of an exclusive licence, or they may restrict the sales of the licensee to certain markets or to certain amounts. They may fix prices, or they may introduce a condition that the licensee should refrain from using other patents for the same class of product. Some firms holding patents have agreements with one another about inter-licensing or about the pooling of their rights. These agreements may prohibit the licensing of outsiders. They may give exclusive rights in particular markets to one of the parties, or they may allot the markets to be served by the members. In all such cases the legal sanctions associated with the grant of patents are used for restrictive purposes similar to those of the classical type of cartel.

Patent agreements are frequently associated with other restrictive arrangements and with inter-locking financial interests. They may thus serve to strengthen the monopoly enjoyed by the members of a cartel or combine. Whether the qualified monopoly conferred by the patent system is necessary, for realizing the purposes for which that system was devised, has been frequently debated and does not concern us here. But the extension of the monopoly by restrictive agreements among patent holders and licensees raises questions which are certainly within the limits of our subject.[1]

Close combines, single-firm monopolies, or monopolies of scale were once commonly described as trusts. This term was originally used, however, for a particular form of organization common in the United States during the latter years of the nineteenth century and the early years of this century. A Voting Trust, as it was then called, was formed when the shares of a group of independent concerns were assigned to a common body of trustees. The shareholders received in exchange trust certificates which entitled them to dividends, control over the policy of the whole group being henceforth vested in the trustees. This form of monopolistic

[1] It is commonly supposed that patents are occasionally taken out by firms for the purpose of suppressing inventions so as to protect existing investments. Such cases seem to be very rare. But serious damage may be caused when, as sometimes happens, large firms threaten progressive newcomers to their trade with actions for patent infringement, even when they are unjustified in doing so. In order to avoid the heavy expense of a patent action, a small firm may then be deterred from going ahead with its innovation.

organization has never been of much significance in Great Britain, and even in the United States, where it originated, it succumbed to a legal attack many decades ago.

The purposes of the trust, however, were often achieved in other ways. One method was that by which concerns became linked through the exchange of shares, as when in 1930 each of the two steel companies created a number of 'liaison ordinary shares' and allotted these to the other. Wherever this happens, the common interest so created helps to ensure the pursuit of a common policy and also loyalty to any other mutual agreements. Many firms which retain an independent existence exchange shares or invest in each other's shares with the same purpose in mind. Similarly they may appoint directors in common. These financial or personal links are often created to strengthen other agreements either for market sharing or for the exchange of technical information and the inter-licensing of patents. Of course, the creation of links of this kind frequently stops short of the point at which the independence of the parties is jeopardized. For instance, although the Imperial Tobacco Company owned 45 per cent of the shares of Gallaher, its leading rival, the former denied that the holding was used to influence the policy of the latter. During the post-war period the import of new techniques from the more advanced to the developing countries has sometimes been accomplished by agreements for technical co-operation, and these are generally accompanied by some investment by the donor company in the recipient company without destroying the latter's independence.

The effects of these financial and personal links, therefore, differ widely from case to case. The same is true of the holding company, the most common type of close combine. The holding company is usually established solely for the purpose of acquiring sufficient shares in other firms to confer on it control over their policy. The subsidiary firms retain their legal identities and sometimes even their administrative and marketing independence, but their policies are brought into conformity with the interests of the group as a whole. The advantage of the holding company for promoters is that it is easy to establish and flexible in its organization. Through this medium a large quantity of capital assets can be controlled through a comparatively small investment, and a dominant position in the market may be secured. Provided that the holding company owns the bare majority of the shares in another company, it can dictate policy. Control can indeed be secured with an even smaller proportion of the total capital when the capital structure of the subsidiaries includes a substantial amount of non-voting shares. The subsidiary companies themselves may control subsidiaries by the same device, and thus a great inverted pyramid of capital interests can be constructed and controlled by a small group. The extent to which this power is used differs widely in practice. Sometimes it is exercised to the full over the whole range of interests covered. On the other hand, some of the groups are loosely knit administratively and the central holding company may leave its subsidiaries with a large measure of autonomy.

Finally, there is the consolidation or merger in which the formerly independent businesses lose their separate existence and a complete fusion of interests is secured. These mergers may be vertical as well as horizontal. Thus, large firms sometimes absorb suppliers or customer firms in order to deny sources of supply or markets to rivals, or in order to avoid the operations of cartels that may restrict their own development, or simply in order to secure technical and commercial economies. The vast majority of mergers, however, both horizontal and vertical, have only slender connections with monopoly. Large growing firms often take over small firms in difficulties or branches of production which firms are surrendering in the course of modifying their interests. The growth of Lucas, the electrical components firm, during the inter-war period was attended by many such mergers in which the initiative frequently came from the directors of the absorbed firm. This type of merger can scarcely be regarded as a means for destroying competition; it is the civilized alternative to the bankruptcy of the failing competitor.[1] On the other hand, some

[1] Cf. D. Dewey, loc. cit., p. 257.

mergers, whether based on a search for market domination or the economies of scale, have undoubtedly led to the replacement of competition by monopoly or quasi-monopoly. In large-scale industry, monopoly in one sector tends to breed monopoly elsewhere. For instance, the establishment of market dominance by a firm, or by a group of associated firms, may encourage combination among supplying or customer firms for the purpose of enhancing their countervailing power. Finally, close combines may be the preferred alternative to cartels in countries where the latter are subjected to legal disabilities. The various devices by which a close combine may be brought into existence need not detain us any longer. What is important from the present point of view is not the path to single-firm monopoly nor its precise structure, but the extent of its dominance and the policy it follows.

The discussion so far has indicated that however clear-cut the concept of monopoly may be in theory, in practice it is somewhat elusive. One reason for this is that a similarity of organization among industries often conceals wide diversities in the degree of market power, while even the possession of a broadly similar degree of market power may accompany different policies in regard to its exercise. Consequently, a study of industrial organization carries us only a short distance along the path to an understanding of monopoly. Undoubtedly, when production is in few hands, there is an a priori expectation that monopoly power exists, whereas when an industry is composed of numerous independent firms it is evident that one of the conditions of vigorous competition is satisfied. Yet, in practice, many examples can be found of concentrated industries in which competition thrives and of multi-firm industries in which it remains weak. This suggests that we must look at the market rather than at the organization of industry for any final assessment of business behaviour. This proposition, however, must not be pressed too far. Organization should not be ignored in a study of monopoly, and most official enquiries undertaken under monopoly legislation take it as a starting point. Evidence of the extent to which production is concentrated may not of itself carry us to our destination, but it cannot be neglected in reaching judgments about the economic effects of particular types of close combine.

Information about concentration is contained in the reports of successive Censuses of Production. These enable us to measure, with fair accuracy, phenomena with which other evidence has made us generally familiar. For manufacturing industry as a whole, the main conclusion is that the vast majority of firms are very small, but that a few large firms are responsible for a very high proportion of the total employment or output. In 1958 there were in Great Britain about 25,000 manufacturing enterprises employing more than twenty-five persons each, but 1,950 of them, employing 500 persons or over, provided 64 per cent of the total employment and over 68 per cent of the total net output, while seventy-four enterprises, employing over 10,000 persons, provided 25 per cent of the employment and 28 per cent of the net output. An 'enterprise', as defined by the Census, consists of one or more firms under common ownership or control as defined by the Companies Act of 1948. Since a firm's effective control over others is often secured even when its financial holdings in its subsidiaries are much smaller than is necessary to satisfy the definition of the Companies Act, concentration of control is, in reality, greater than these figures suggest. This is the position for manufacturing industry as a whole. It is clear that policy-making decisions for a large part of British industry rest with relatively few boards of directors.

The degree of concentration varies widely from industry to industry. It is commonly expressed by giving the employment or output of the three largest enterprises in industry as a proportion of the total employment or output in that industry. In 1958 the concentration ratios, as they are called, were 84 per cent for oil refining, 60 per cent for soap and detergents, 81 per cent for man-made fibres and 70 per cent for watches and clocks, whereas they were only 8 per cent for hosiery, 9 per cent for woollen and worsted textiles, 12 per cent for pottery and 15 per cent for furniture. These figures refer to employment. Concentration ratios based on net output are shown in the following table:

Industry	*Percentage of Net Output*
Man-made fibres	89
Oil refining	88
Sugar	79
Soap and detergents	69
Watches and clocks	65
Cement	70
Tobacco	81
Motor vehicles	47
Pottery	15
Leather goods	9
Woollen and worsted	8
Hosiery	9
Furniture	8
Printing and publishing	8

Similar tables have been compiled for other industrial countries. Although they show a comparable divergence between industries, for the same industries the ratios differ from country to country. These differences depend on a number of causes, such as factor-endowments, the relative sizes of the economies in the comparison, varying Census definitions of the same industries, and possibly the attitude of the law towards concentration. Attempts have also been made to compare changes in concentration over time. For this country such comparisons are difficult because of the lack of an adequate statistical basis and because of changes in methods of classification. The recent work of investigators, however, refutes the commonly held view that there is an inevitable trend towards concentration in modern economies. It has been suggested that 'the extent to which many [British] industries are dominated by a few giant enterprises seems to be increasing', but this conclusion is tentative and does not apply universally.[1] In the United States the trend appears to have been in the opposite direction in the last few decades.

These statistical results have a limited value for the study of monopoly. The enterprises are classified according to their chief product, and the ratios may consequently give a misleading impression for multi-product enterprises, unless the whole output is closely related. Again, the same ratio may have a different significance according to the size of the individual shares of the three largest firms. In one industry the firms may be equally matched rivals, in another industry one of the firms may be vastly greater than the other two. The degree of concentration also depends closely on the type of classification adopted. For textiles as a whole the concentration ratio is low; for some types of textile products (e.g. acrylic fibres) it is very high. The chief disadvantage of concentration ratios as a measure of monopoly arises from the fact that it is concerned with industrial organization and results from approaching the problem from the side of supply. Monopoly and competition are, however, market phenomena, and unless we know something of the elasticity of substitution between products, concentration ratios are not very helpful. For example, industries with low concentration ratios may show strong monopolistic features because firms in them enjoy local monopolies that result from high transport costs, whereas industries with high concentration ratios may sometimes be exposed to keen competition from close substitutes produced by other industries. The linoleum industry is highly concentrated, but the market for floor coverings, which is served by numerous firms in the carpet, felt, rubber and plastics industries, is keenly competitive. Moreover, concentration ratios tell us nothing about the extent to which competition is restrained by agreements among independent firms.

Nevertheless, these data are not worthless for the study of

[1] A. Armstrong and A. Silberston, 'Size of Plant, Size of Enterprise and Concentration on British Manufacturing Industry, 1935–58' in *Journal of the Royal Statistical Society*, vol. 128, part 3, 1965, p. 405.

monopoly. It will be seen later that the British Government in selecting its references to the Monopolies Commission has been influenced by the extent of concentration in the various industries that are candidates for enquiry, and also that the Monopolies Commission itself has always begun its investigations by studying the facts of organization. The Monopolies and Restrictive Practices Act of 1948 requires that, before an enquiry can proceed, the Commission must satisfy itself that a monopoly exists, and a monopoly is there defined by reference to the proportion of the industry's output that is in the hands of either a single firm or a group of firms bound by restrictive arrangements. This is a reasonable requirement. In spite of all the qualifications mentioned, it is generally true that effective restrictions on competition can be imposed more easily when the market is served by a small number of firms than when there are many. Thus, although concentration ratios cannot carry us very far in our study, they assist in the first steps of the inquiry.

CHAPTER IV

The Historical and Legal Background in the United Kingdom

I

A HISTORICAL SURVEY

It is sometimes supposed that the nineteenth century saw a strong and persistent trend towards monopoly. An economic system based on *laissez faire* and free competition was steadily in retreat, so it is vaguely believed, and monopoly thus extended its sway over an ever-widening area of industry. This belief has even slenderer justification than the notion, criticized in the last chapter, that during the present century there has been a strong and inevitable tendency towards greater concentration. If we are to reach a just opinion in these matters we must first clarify the meaning of *laissez faire*, which in popular discussion is often identified with free competition.

The term *laissez faire* refers to public policy towards economic activity. Some writers have used it to describe a doctrine based on the proposition that the State should confine its economic functions to such matters as the maintenance of a stable currency system and the enforcement of contracts and that it should leave the ordering of economic affairs to the decisions of individuals in a free market. This doctrine is ascribed to the classical economists and it is widely believed to have been followed by the governments of this country during the middle years of the nineteenth century. It is, in fact, questionable whether the leading classical economists placed such narrow limits on State action. On the contrary, there is evidence for the view that, while they believed in the virtues of a free market economy, they were well aware that government interference was often necessary to maintain such an economy intact. The neo-classical economists of the Cambridge school went further and argued that under unrestricted private enterprise the distribution of resources was liable to be distorted because producers could sometimes throw on to others some part of the costs which their operations entailed.[1] Government interference was thus sometimes necessary in order to promote the optimum allocation of resources and the efficient conduct of economic affairs under private enterprise. It is, therefore, sensible to regard *laissez faire* as a policy directed towards maintaining or developing a free market economy and at the same time to realize that the public authority is often obliged to intervene in economic processes to this end, or to create institutions which will have the desired effect. Areas where competition operates most freely, probably the only areas where it operates perfectly, are those for which the Government, or some corporate body created for the purpose, has introduced regulations deliberately designed to bring about such conditions. Examples are to be found in the produce markets and the stock exchanges. Moreover, the extent to which free competition prevails in any country is powerfully influenced by the disposition of the law towards it and towards its opposite, monopoly. Thus, non-interference by the Government and free competition are not to be equated.

We can now consider the truth of the statement made at the beginning of this chapter. A glance at the industrial history of the country at once throws doubt upon it. In the days when most markets were local, the force of competition was necessarily feeble. Improvements in transport, by the construction first of canals and

[1] These economists drew a distinction between private net product and social net product and showed that these might differ, as when the operations of a factory or mine destroyed amenities and brought additional costs (say, for cleaning) to the surrounding community.

then of railways, greatly enlarged the area of competition and exposed suppliers who hitherto enjoyed a local monopoly to rivalry from outside. This process continued throughout the nineteenth and twentieth centuries with the result that in many classes of goods producers had to face competition from overseas as well as from domestic suppliers. The area of competition was extended not only by the cheapening of the various means of transport and communications, but also by the standardization of many classes of manufactured goods as a result of the replacement of craftsmanship by large-scale productive methods.

When this increased competitive pressure was felt by the established suppliers, they frequently tried to meet it by concerted action. In other words, restrictive practices were often adopted as a response to the intensification of competition for the purpose of preserving the *status quo*. Nor are the devices employed by manufacturers of the present generation of recent origin. Many types of restrictive practices encountered in modern times can find their parallel earlier on. For instance, the organization of the copper mining industry of Cornwall towards the end of the eighteenth century passed through the familiar stages of minimum price agreements, quotas on sales, central selling arrangements and even membership of an international cartel. The Newcastle Coal Vend is a well-known example of a powerful and long-lived cartel that flourished in what is regarded as the hey-day of industrial individualism. Price agreements in the iron and textile trades were common in the nineteenth century, especially during periods of bad trade. Not all these arrangements were successful, for with technical innovation and ever-widening sources of supply, competitive pressures tended to increase and were sometimes irresistible. But it seems that, in all periods when conditions have been favourable, producers have tried to safeguard their interests by restrictive arrangements.

For trades that served local markets the number of members involved in these arrangements was naturally small. But an increasing number of cartels during the later years of the nineteenth century covered national markets and, when opportunity offered, national producers did not hesitate to join with those in other countries in efforts to restrain competition. For example, in 1883 the rail makers of Britain, Germany and Belgium formed an International Rail Syndicate. This allotted orders in agreed shares among the several national groups which in turn determined the quotas for individual works. Early in the new century the French and the American rail makers became members of the Syndicate. In the shipping industry numerous cartels, known as Conferences, were formed to regulate the liner trades on the busiest ocean routes.

As long as manufacturing industry was conducted predominantly by small- or medium-sized family businesses, cartels were naturally the favoured device for limiting competition. The later years of the nineteenth century, however, saw the growth of many large companies, and conditions became favourable for a combination movement which led to the emergence of great dominating concerns in several industries. During the decades immediately before the First World War this movement had achieved conspicuous results in the soap, salt-mining, match, tobacco, whisky, wallpaper and cement industries and in several branches of chemicals, e.g. alkali and explosives. The main branches of the staple industries, however, coal, iron and steel, shipbuilding and textiles, remained very competitive, but even they provided, in certain of their more highly specialized branches, many examples of monopoly. In the textile finishing trades and in the manufacture of sewing thread powerful combines were built up, and in the anthracite coal trade and in several branches of the iron and steel and the finished metal industries cartels operated with varied success.

Despite these tendencies, it is probable that before the First World War British industry as a whole could claim to be more highly competitive than German or American industry. Several reasons may be adduced. A high proportion of the output of the staple British industries was sold in foreign markets where restraints over competition were difficult or impossible to impose.

At the same time the adherence of Great Britain to its traditional free trade policy meant that the home market was exposed to foreign competition and that the price-fixing efforts of cartels were likely to be defeated by imports. Moreover, it cannot be too strongly emphasized when one is considering the prevalence of monopoly that it is not the number nor the coverage of cartels that exercises the most decisive influence, nor even the presence of great firms in particular industries, but rather the power that these organizations are able to exert over the market. In the conditions that existed in Great Britain before the First World War, many cartels led a precarious existence. Even the policy of apparently dominant firms was in many industries affected by the ease with which rivals from other countries could move into the British market.

The First World War and the accompanying inflation weakened the defences of the competitive system. The Committee on Trusts and the Committees of Enquiry established under the Profiteering Acts of 1919–20 were both impressed with the wide extent of arrangements for price-fixing. During the 1920s, however, the staple industries became chronically depressed, and their profits were adversely affected by an increasing surplus of capacity and by the bitter competition that attended it. The attempts of firms to restrain this competition by cartelization were largely ineffective until towards the end of the decade when the Government took a hand. By then both industrialists and politicians had been persuaded that only by rationalization, which required concerted efforts by all members of an industry, could the surplus capacity be removed and profitability restored. Some of the schemes that were introduced at this time provided for consolidation within an industry and the elimination of surplus plant, while others took the form of arrangements for fixing minimum prices and allotting quotas. During the next decade the Government enforced cartelization by law in some industries, as in coalmining and in agriculture. In other industries, e.g. wool-combing and shipbuilding, rationalization was financed by the semi-official Bankers' Industrial Development Company and assisted by tax concessions. Some British producers now began to take a more important part than formerly in international cartels, and in this they often received encouragement from the Government, notably in the case of the iron and steel industry. Meanwhile, the practice of resale price maintenance became more widely extended, and in several industries elaborate arrangements for the joint enforcement of the resale prices fixed by individual manufacturers were devized.

Combines and cartels were not confined to the decaying industries. During the inter-war period great dominating combines appeared in the iron and steel, chemical, grain milling, rayon, electrical apparatus and motor accessory industries, while cartels became very widespread especially after the final abandonment of the free trade policy in 1932. By the outbreak of the Second World War it is probable that the majority of the leading British industries were familiar with devices for restricting competition, and public and official opinion had veered round in favour of monopoly and its familiar associate, planning. In the deflationary conditions of the period, however, the power of the producers to determine prices remained narrowly limited, except in the important instances where monopoly was supported by law or by official administrative arrangements that had the same effect.

The Second World War greatly strengthened the trend towards monopoly. Trade associations and dominant firms were used as agents of government policy, and the official control imposed over imports, production, manufacturing resources and prices reduced competitive pressures. In many of the plans put forward towards the end of the war by trade associations in preparation for the coming of peace, and in much of the Government's own thinking about post-war industrial organization, it was assumed that free competition would play a minor part in the ordering of the economy. The business leaders and civil servants then in positions of authority had been reared in an era of depression. In the main they were defeatist in their attitude towards British industry's chance of thriving in the period that lay ahead, and they thought in terms of defensive measures to safeguard markets for established suppliers. Britain's economic failures in the post-war world may be attributable in some degree to the persistence of several years of this pessimistic outlook among the men in control of industry and government. May it not be significant that in the country which has made the most rapid economic advance since the war (Japan), the older leaders in industry and government were for the most part purged in 1945 by order of the Occupying Power? It is true that the British Government was persuaded to interest itself in monopolies and restrictive practices immediately after the war, but its policy for a long time faltered in the face of opposition and scepticism from both politicians and industrialists.

2

THE LEGAL BACKGROUND

Until 1948 when the Monopolies and Restrictive Practices (Inquiry and Control) Act was passed, there was no modern statute law in Great Britain regarding monopoly in general. This does not mean that the State had been indifferent to particular manifestations of monopoly. For instance, the patent law had for centuries governed the conditions for the grant of a qualified monopoly to patentees. Then, with the growing importance during the latter half of the nineteenth century of certain industries that fell into the class of public utilities, official regulation was imposed over the sector. The private Acts of Parliament, under which the early railways were built and which conferred on the railway companies the right to acquire land compulsorily, prescribed maximum charges for different classes of traffic and imposed other obligations on the companies. In 1888 the Railway and Canal Traffic Act conferred on the Board of Trade the power of classifying rates and set up a judicial body (the Railway and Canal Commission) to administer the Act. Subsequent legislation introduced other measures of rate control, and the Railways Act of 1921 provided for a system of standard charges and exceptional rates. It also established the

Railway Rates Tribunal to review the charges. Again, the private Acts of Parliament which conferred on the early gas companies rights over the public domain, likewise regulated their prices and profits. Subsequently there was general legislation which defined the circumstances under which discriminatory prices might be charged. Similar measures of control were imposed over the charges of the electricity supply companies.

All these industries fell into the category of 'natural monopolies'. They were industries in which the competitive restraint on the exploitation of consumers was necessarily absent, partly because the unit of production was generally coterminous with the market served, and partly because the companies needed the right of using the public domain which could not be given unreservedly. The principles commonly applied by the Government in exerting control were fairly clear. Prices and profits were limited in order to prevent the exploitation of consumers. The circumstances in which discriminatory prices might be charged were regulated in order to prevent unfairness between different customers. Undue preference was forbidden for the same reason and so was the right to refuse service to would-be customers. Some public utilities soon passed under the ownership and control of municipalities, and public control reached its logical conclusion after the Second World War with the nationalization of the railways and of the electricity and gas industries.

In the inter-war period government supervision over other industries was extended. In the nineteen-twenties official bodies were set up to survey and report on the prices of building materials and food, and, later, with the compulsory cartelization of certain industries, statutory committees were given the responsibility of dealing with complaints from customers. In the nineteen-thirties the Import Duties Advisory Committee, established originally to advise the Government on proposals to increase import duties, came to exercise a general supervision over prices in the steel industry, a function that in the Second World War was discharged by the Iron and Steel Board.

All these could be regarded as special cases. Monopolies and restrictive practices in manufacturing industry and trade were, with these exceptions, virtually free from control. The common law, if not as active as is commonly supposed in encouraging them, did nothing to restrain them in recent times. A survey of the evolution of common law doctrines in regard to monopoly, conspiracy and the restraint of trade lies beyond the scope of this book. All that need be said here is that during the century which preceded the passing of the Monopolies and Restrictive Practices Act of 1948 the Courts appear to have played a part of steadily decreasing importance in the maintenance of competitive conditions. Indeed the original hostility of the common law changed to tolerance. Thus, in regard to conspiracy, Lord Mansfield, in his famous judgment in Rex v. Eccles of 1783, had declared: 'Persons in possession of any articles of trade may sell them at such prices as they individually please, but if they confederate and agree not to sell them, it is conspiracy.' In the middle of the nineteenth century, when booksellers contemplated forming a price-fixing association, they gave up the project on receiving counsel's opinion that, if carried out, it would render them liable to prosecution for criminal conspiracy.

This legal position was undermined by a series of Court decisions during the second half of the nineteenth century. In this period legislation was passed to protect trade unions against actions for conspiracy, and it seems that the Courts were inclined to accord the same protection to businessmen. In 1892, in the celebrated Mogul case, the judges accepted the doctrine 'that one may do anything to get rid of a business rival provided that one does not commit a well-defined tort'. The Trades Disputes Act of 1906, which was, of course, primarily concerned with defining permissible actions by trade unions in trade disputes, had the general effect of affirming the main principles enunciated in the Mogul case. Henceforth, actions for conspiracy against an association of traders who sought to damage the business of a rival could succeed only if they were actuated by 'disinterested malevolence', that is to say, if their conspiracy was inspired simply by malice.

The original doctrine of the non-enforcement of contracts in restraint of trade suffered a similar erosion. Agreements in restraint of trade, according to the principles enunciated in the Nordenfeldt case of 1892, were void and unenforceable unless they were shown to be reasonable both between the parties and in relation to the public interest. But the Courts in practice were disinclined to set aside properly drawn contracts on grounds that the public interest was offended, largely because the judges were reluctant to assess evidence on an economic character. The Courts were, in fact, seldom called upon to enforce 'reasonable' cartel agreements, since trade associations preferred to rely upon private methods for ensuring adherence to their rules. In the twenty years before the Second World War, the most important cases of this character had their origin in the efforts of trade associations to enforce collective resale price maintenance. On the whole, the Courts were unwilling to protect traders against such efforts, but some uncertainty remained until it was removed in 1937 by a decision of the House of Lords. A plaintiff had contended that it was unlawful for the Motor Trade Association to fine or to put his name on a Stop List because he had sold a car at other than the list price. The Court rejected this contention. Thus, although in modern times the common law did not actively promote monopolies and restrictive practices, it certainly placed no obstacles in their way. In Great Britain, combinations and cartels could be established and restrictive practices introduced without legal restraint, in marked contrast to the position in the United States and some other countries.

It cannot be said that public opinion was disturbed by this legal attitude. In the still highly competitive economy of the period before 1914 the danger of monopolistic exploitation appeared to be very small. Since at that time the staple industries were expanding, charges of technical stagnation or inefficiency could not in any event be pressed home. On the other hand, in the inter-war period, deflationary conditions and the chronic depression of the great industries removed any danger of exploitation on the part of management. Indeed, during that period cartels themselves were necessarily inclined to caution in their price-fixing policies. The danger to the public interest seemed to lie in the persistence of unprofitable price levels which left producers with insufficient resources for modernizing their equipment. The Government's policy of encouraging the cartelization or rationalization of the most hard-pressed industries was on the whole applauded by the public. In these circumstances it was not to be expected that the Courts in their judgments on monopolies and restrictive practices should reach decisions contrary to the prevailing trend.

CHAPTER V

The Genesis of British Monopoly Policy

We have observed that during the inter-war period the Courts, the Government and public opinion had become increasingly well-disposed towards measures for restricting competition. To a large extent this trend was a consequence of the industrial depression when cartels, unless buttressed by government power, were insecure and when agreed price structures were precarious. Whether the policy had merits even in such circumstances is debatable. It was clearly likely to be inappropriate to an era of high demand and full employment.

This point was evident to those concerned towards the end of the Second World War with framing post-war policy. In 1943 the Board of Trade set up a department to survey the problems of post-war reconstruction, and attention in that department was soon directed towards monopoly and restrictive practices. It was incontestable that, unless British industry could raise its efficiency and expand its sales to foreign markets, there could be little hope of social progress, for the large net income formerly received from foreign investments was no longer available. The pre-war industrial policy of market-sharing and price-maintenance was certainly not conducive to the continuous improvements in methods now required. The aim of maintaining the *status quo*, it seemed, must yield to that of ensuring a ready transference of production from high-cost to low-cost producers under the stimulus of competition. These, at any rate, were the principles that persuaded a group of temporary civil servants, then concerned with post-war reconstruction, to draw up their recommendations for a full-blooded anti-monopoly policy. The permanent officials of the Board of Trade, who had fathered the restrictive policies of the 1930s, were not easily convinced of the merits of such a break with the past, and in any case had little faith in the virtues of competition. The arguments for a change in policy, however, were reinforced when the Government accepted a full-employment policy which was set out in the famous White Paper of 1944.[1] In that document it was argued that measures for the maintenance of effective demand might lead, in the presence of widespread monopoly and restrictive practices, to higher prices and profits rather than to enlarged output and greater employment. So, since a full-employment policy to which all political parties were committed might be frustrated by the actions of private monopolists, a new attitude was called for.

Had it not been for this association of the full-employment policy with anti-monopoly measures, it is doubtful if the resistance to change would have been overcome. The established civil servants were almost all suspicious of the new proposals and the politicians in both parties were divided in their opinions. In general, Labour ministers brought up on Socialist doctrines saw little merit in free competition, and the Marxists among them thought of monopoly as a stage on the road to the State ownership of productive resources. Many trade union leaders, like Ernest Bevin, knew by experience, that monopolies and cartels were more amenable to trade union pressure than firms subject to the discipline of the market. Industry at this time was strong in its advocacy of Enabling Acts which would confer on representative bodies coercive powers over all members of an industry. It viewed proposals to regulate monopoly with hostility, and the public itself showed little interest in the controversy. It may be that murmurs from the United States Government, then in a mood of renewed liberalism, exerted some influence. That Government was actively concerning itself with the operations of international cartels and was pressing other governments for indications of their policies in regard to them. Inquiries

[1] White Paper on *Employment Policy*, Cmd. 6527, 1944.

by the British Government into those cartels, and the official attitude towards British participants in them, could hardly be dissociated from policy towards monopoly and restrictive practices as a whole. Something had to be done.

Soon after the end of the war most of those who had advocated a vigorous anti-monopoly policy had left government service, and the field remained in possession of lukewarm supporters or opponents. This, together with the continuing hostility of industry, meant that there could be no question of mounting an attack on monopolies and restrictive practices on American lines. Indeed, in view of the weight of opposition and suspicion, it is remarkable that the Act of 1948 went as far as it did. This was, after all, the first statute in modern times to deal with these questions in a general economic context. Apart from the fact that it came at the end of a long period in which monopoly and restrictive practices had been in favour, there was ignorance in nearly all circles about what was involved.

As the full title of the Act shows, the Government and Parliament were primarily concerned with instituting inquiries into industries where monopoly was thought to exist. They sought also to elicit judgments about whether the conditions found to prevail were contrary to the public interest. In effect, they seemed to declare, rather disingenuously: 'We are ignorant in this country about the extent of monopolies and restrictive practices and about their economic effects. At present we have no means of discovering whether those effects are good or bad. But we believe that where monopoly is found to exist, it should be investigated and its effects assessed by an impartial tribunal.' The tribunal set up by the Act was the Monopolies and Restrictive Practices Commission. Its membership consisted of persons with a diversity of experience presumed to be appropriate to its functions, namely businessmen, accountants, lawyers, economists, trade unionists and ex-civil servants. All these were part-time members, except for the chairman, the secretary (a permanent civil servant) and, initially, one other person. The Commission was provided with a staff of investigators, some of them seconded from government departments and others specially recruited.

The Commission was not empowered to take the initiative in instituting inquiries; these could begin only after the Government had referred cases to it. In the selection of references the Government was naturally influenced by its conception of the Commission's primary function. This was to provide a body of evidence about monopolies and restrictive practices which would guide the Government in framing its policy in the years ahead. The Board of Trade, the sponsoring department from which the Commission received its references, stated explicitly in its annual report for 1953 that the choice of subjects for inquiry was strongly affected by this consideration. The criteria employed were, it added, the nature of the industry and of its trade practices and the volume of representations made to the Board. Particular choices, however, were often determined by pressure exerted in Parliament or by the public after allegations had been made about the charging of excessive prices. One effect of this was that the Commission's time was sometimes dissipated in what were trivial investigations from the stand-point of policy-making. By no means all the industries selected were of substantial importance to the economy, and the same types of practice were repeatedly investigated in different industries. It is probable that if the Commission had been given power to make its own selection of cases, its work would have been more effective. However, this is being wise after the event. The Commission came into existence in a formative phase of monopoly policy, and the Government was inexperienced in this field. The early references themselves indicated that some effort was made to cover a fairly representative sample of British industry. A list of the references appears opposite.

These reports, in addition to a general report entitled 'Collective Discrimination', were all completed (though not necessarily published) before the Restrictive Trade Practices Act of 1956 came into force. The subsequent career of the Monopolies Commission (from 1956 to the present time) is described in Chapter IX.

Reference	*Date of the Report*
Dental Goods	1950
Cast Iron Rain Water Goods	1951
Electric Lamps	1951
Insulated Electric Wires and Cables	1952
Insulin	1952
Matches and Match-Making Machinery	1953
Imported Timber	1953
Calico Printing	1954
London Building Industry	1954
Semi-Manufactures of Copper and Copper Alloys	1955
Pneumatic Tyres	1955
Sand and Gravel in Central Scotland	1956
Hard Fibre Cordage	1956
Linoleum	1956
Rubber Footwear	1956
Industrial Gases	1957
Electrical and Allied Machinery and Plant	1957
Electric Valves and Cathode Ray Tubes	1957
Tea	1957
Standard Metal Windows	1957

The conditions which the Commission was required to investigate applied to the supply of goods for home and export and to the application of any process to goods. Services, the professions, the nationalized industries and the trade unions were explicitly excluded. Monopoly was defined as a condition in which at least one-third of the goods was supplied by a single firm or by two or more firms with arrangements with one another that had the effect of restricting competition. Here was a rough and ready definition of monopoly.[1]

When the Commission received a reference, its first task was to determine whether the condition of monopoly as defined in the Act existed. If not, the enquiry could proceed no further. If, as was

[1] See Appendix A(i).

usually the case, monopoly was found to exist, then the Commission was required to investigate the practices of the trade, to report on the extent to which these practices (or 'things done', in the words of the Act) were the result of the monopoly or were used for the purpose of preserving the monopoly. The next step was to decide whether the 'things done' operated or might be expected to operate against the public interest and, if necessary, to suggest remedies.[1] Every report, when complete, was sent to the Board of Trade for submission to Parliament. Further action was the responsibility of the Board of Trade which had the authority to issue an Order, subject to Parliamentary resolution, to require the suppliers to desist from some or all of the practices adversely reported on.

Since the Commission's decision in any reference was supposed to depend on its judgment of how the public interest was affected, one might have expected that the Act would provide a definition of that concept. In fact, the guidance given by the Act consisted of a string of platitudes which the Commission found valueless, and it was left for the members themselves to reach their own conclusions by reference to the assumptions, principles or prejudices which their training and experience caused them to apply to economic affairs.[2] This common-sense method of dealing with a difficult problem proved to be reasonably satisfactory, at any rate as an initial approach. In this context the public interest probably defied legal definition. The Commission was being asked to discover the economic effects of certain kinds of business conduct and to judge whether that conduct was damaging to economic welfare. If a group of responsible people with a diversity of training and experience was able to reach agreed conclusions on these matters, it was reasonable to suppose that those conclusions would conform to what was generally acceptable. In the event, the Commission was usually successful in reaching agreed judgments about the

[1] The Commission might be asked to limit its enquiries to the discovery of the facts; in such a case it would not proceed to consider whether the practices or conditions were contrary to the public interest.

[2] See Appendix A(ii) for section of Act dealing with the public interest.

impact of particular practices upon the public interest. Most of their disagreements, as shown in the minority reports, turned on the expediency of the remedies.

The process of enquiry and report proved to be lengthy, and two-and-a-half years usually elapsed between the receipt of a reference and the presentation of the report. However, the Commission usually found itself engaged upon several enquiries at the same time, and in the course of seven years (1949–55) it completed twenty reports.[1] Speedier progress was hampered by the part-time character of the membership and also by the Commission's insistence upon making detailed historical enquiries and upon securing a substantial measure of agreement with the firms investigated concerning the facts. The necessity for the historical enquiry, which some critics questioned, was derived from the provision in the Act that the Commission should consider not only whether the business practices under investigation operated against the public interest, but also whether they might be expected so to operate. It was held that only by examination of past activities and policies was it possible for the Commission to fulfil this requirement.

On receiving a reference the Commission and its secretariat first proceeded to gather facts which would show whether the goods covered were supplied under the conditions to which the Act applied, that is, whether the suppliers were monopolists according to the legal definition. The next step was to obtain from all available sources, such as the records of the firms and the evidence of outsiders (including that of rival firms and customers), information about past and present practices, that is to say, the 'things done' as a result of the monopoly or for the purpose of maintaining it. When the Commission thought that it had obtained adequate information, it held a 'clarification hearing' with the firms or associations for the purpose of ensuring that its understanding of the facts was correct, or at any rate undisputed. The next stage involved the formation

[1] An amending Act, passed in 1953, increased the maximum size of the Commission from ten to twenty-five and allowed the Commission to work in panels.

of tentative judgments about whether any of the 'things done' offended, or were likely to offend, the public interest. These were discussed at a 'public interest' hearing with the trade. At this meeting the trade was given the opportunity of answering criticisms of any of its practices which, in the Commission's provisional view, were open to censure. Then the Commission proceeded to reach its final conclusions on these matters, to consider recommendations about what should be done to deal with the practices to which it took exception, and to draft and present its report. Most investigations included an enquiry by accountants into costs, prices and profits, for the reasonableness or otherwise of the profits earned was naturally believed to have a bearing on the problems to which the Commission addressed its attention.

It is important to observe that the Act imputed no vice to monopoly or restrictive practices as such. Where monopoly was found to exist, the public interest, so it was held, required that the trade should be investigated. But there was no assumption in the Act that free competition was necessarily preferable to monopoly, except in the sense that only trades in which monopoly existed[1] were subject to inquiry. Nor was it to be considered that the firms producing the goods chosen for reference were in any sense on trial. 'To monopolize' was no offence under the law. The Commission's investigations were simply directed towards discovering the economic effects of certain practices and suggesting what should be done if those effects were found to be socially undesirable. Further, the Commission was not concerned to judge whether the trade was conducting its affairs efficiently, but only with reaching conclusions about whether *certain practices* led to inefficiency by impeding improvements in methods and by wasting resources.

The Monopolies and Restrictive Practices Act was not the only expression of post-war concern with this subject. The report of the post-war Swan Committee on Patents was followed by an amended Patents Act of 1949 which further qualified the monopoly granted to patentees. The main purpose of patent legislation is to encourage

[1] In the legal sense, that is.

invention and the development of inventions by bestowing the privilege of a temporary monopoly on those who file patents. Critics of this policy have suggested that the monopoly so granted is unduly restrictive. They have argued that inventors would be adequately encouraged if all patents were endorsed 'licences of right', and if their income were to be derived from royalties payable by anyone who chose to use the patent. These arguments did not convince the Swan Committee or Parliament, but the Patents Act of 1949 conferred on the Comptroller of the Patent Office greater powers than formerly for granting licences of right in cases where inventions were not being adequately exploited or where the monopoly was being abused. These powers were related to the activities of the Monopolies Commission. Where the Commission found that the use of patent rights contributed to practices deemed by them socially undesirable, the Comptroller of the Patent Office could take this conclusion into account in deciding whether to give licences of right.

The Government also showed its concern with restrictive practices by instituting other enquiries into industries where the actions of monopolists had attracted public criticism. Building materials were investigated by a special committee in 1948, radio valves by the Central Price Regulation Committee in 1946, and the whole problem of resale price maintenance by the Lloyd Jacob Committee which reported in 1949. By no means all the activities of the Government at this time were consistent, but it had at last been recognized that the presence of monopoly and restrictive practices in British industry raised problems which, if not solved, might seriously hamper economic progress. The Government still remained in doubt about the principles that should inform its policy, and the minds of businessmen, when directed towards the problems that lay ahead, still harked back to the expedients of the 1930s. Consequently, it was probably inevitable that a long period of inquiry and debate should elapse before any definite policy hostile to monopoly and restrictive practices could be devised that commanded any wide acceptance.

CHAPTER VI

The Monopolies Commission

The industries investigated by the Commission differed widely in their organization. In some of them production was in the hands of numerous firms none of which had a sufficiently large share of the market to warrant its being classified as a monopolist in its own right according to the legal definition. The hard fibre cordage industry, building, and imported timber fell into this class. At the other extreme, there were a few industries in which a single firm occupied a dominant position among other producers, in some instances to the extent of being responsible for nearly all the output. The pneumatic tyre, calico printing, match, industrial and medical gases and metal window industries were in this class.[1] The most populous class, however, comprised industries of the oligopolistic type. In them a large part of the output was in the hands of a small number of concerns which were fairly evenly matched in size (electric lamps, electric cables, dental goods, insulin, valves and tubes and electrical machinery). The three classes thus corresponded fairly closely to the conventional threefold classification of industries into those characterized by competition, monopoly and oligopoly.

The diversity of organization among the industries investigated meant that monopoly (which in the legal sense was found to

[1] In the tyre industry during the early 1950s Dunlop was responsible for 47 per cent of the total sales (by value) of the industry; the Calico Printers' Association Ltd. then had nearly half the total calico printing business. The largest producer in the match, industrial gases and metal window industries was responsible for a much higher proportion than this of the British output of the several products.

prevail in all of them, except tea) was achieved by different routes. In industries of the first class (the multi-firm industries) it resulted from restrictive agreements or cartels, and in industries of the second class from the presence of a dominant firm. In the oligopolistic class the route was less clearly marked. There, one or more firms might be (legal) monopolists in their own right because each supplied a third or more of the output, and the scope of the monopoly thus established might be extended by arrangements with other firms in the industry or by the acceptance of one firm as a price leader. In other oligopolistic industries the monopoly came into being because the firms were associated in some kind of restrictive agreement, formal or informal, or because competition was restricted through the pursuit by individual firms of certain policies, despite the absence of any agreement among the members of the trade. The Commission was empowered to act if, even in the absence of formal agreements, firms so conducted their businesses as to restrict competition.

As we have already seen, the establishment of the fact of monopoly was only the preliminary stage in each enquiry, and this seldom caused any difficulty or dispute between the Commission and the firms investigated. The main attention of the Commission was directed towards the actions of firms which either resulted from the conditions of monopoly or were designed to preserve it. It cannot be too strongly emphasized that it was the actions of firms, the 'things done', which might excite condemnation, not the fact of monopoly as such. Let us then consider these 'things done' as disclosed by the Commission in its reports.

It cannot be claimed that the Commission brought to light many practices of which close students of monopoly were unaware. But it did succeed in demonstrating not only that restrictive practices were widespread in British industry, but also that similar practices were followed by industries of very different types. So, the Commission was able to investigate the economic effects of the same practice in different conditions. For this reason its conclusions about them went far towards establishing the basis of the general principles of control for which the Government was seeking.

The chief restrictive practices considered by the Commission were as follows: exclusive dealing arrangements between manufacturers and distributors which limited the channels of distribution or supply for independent competitors, resale price maintenance and agreements to impose or to enforce resale price maintenance, common pricing arrangements among manufacturers, price discrimination, quota schemes for sharing output or markets, agreements on tendering for contracts, agreements to restrict the access of outside firms to materials or machinery, agreements to limit imports or to control international competition, agreements to restrict the use of patent rights and to discriminate in technical co-operation. Most of these types of restrictive practice obviously depended on formal agreements among several firms, but others could be introduced by a monopolist on his own. The latter included various types of discrimination, e.g. price discrimination and exclusive dealing.

Let us now consider these practices in operation in the industries surveyed. Exclusive dealing arrangements proved to be the practice most frequently encountered for maintaining or strengthening a monopolistic position already established by other means. In the dental goods industry the manufacturer-members of the trade association were required to sell their goods (apart from those sold at retail prices) only through dealer-members, and dealer-members were required to buy exclusively from manufacturer-members. Membership of the association, moreover, was limited. In the cast-iron rainwater goods industry only merchants who undertook to buy exclusively from members of the British Iron Founders' Association received full merchant terms. The members of the Electric Lamp Manufacturers' Association provided supplies of lamps on wholesale terms only to traders who agreed to refrain from selling lamps produced by outside manufacturers. Retailers who signed a corresponding agreement were granted additional discounts. In this trade the dealer also received aggregated rebates based on his total sales of lamps produced by all members of the association. Similar arrangements were found in some branches of the electric wire and cable industries.

If the distributors covered by agreements of this kind comprised the most important outlets for the supplies, then it was made difficult for new firms to reach the market and for existing independent firms to enlarge their business. The arrangement was especially restrictive when limitations were placed on admission to the cartel itself, and when powerful sanctions could be exerted for any breach of the rules. For example, a firm that offended might sometimes be boycotted by other members of the cartel. This meant that, if he were a distributor, he would be deprived of supplies and, if a manufacturer, of distributive channels. Exclusive dealing arrangements were sometimes introduced by single-firm monopolies on their own initiative.

Resale price maintenance and collective arrangements in regard to it were encountered in nearly all the industries which sold a substantial part of their output through retailers. The practice of RPM itself will be considered later, and here we shall deal only with collective arrangements for carrying out that policy. The collective arrangements sometimes provided for the enforcement of common resale prices fixed by the associated manufacturers, as in the cast-iron rainwater goods trade; but more usually they were designed to ensure that the resale prices fixed by individual manufacturers were adhered to. For dental goods every associated manufacturer was obliged to fix resale prices for his goods, and if he failed to do so, the association itself fixed them. The bodies set up by the trades for dealing with RPM sometimes made use of an elaborate procedure for enquiring into alleged offences. A fuller discussion of resale price maintenance and the procedures associated with it is provided in Chapter VIII.

Both exclusive dealing arrangements and collective arrangements for resale price maintenance, together with cognate agreements for loyalty rebates, were concerned with the relations between manufacturer and distributor. They were designed to prevent independent firms from securing access to the market and to strengthen the price-fixing powers of manufacturers and traders. Other arrangements applied solely to relations among manufacturers. The most widespread practice in this class was the fixing of common or minimum prices, which might be delivered prices, ex-work prices or resale prices. Since the primary object of cartels was to eliminate or control price-competition it was to be expected that the Commission would encounter this practice in almost all the industries investigated; the dental goods trade was a notable exception. In order to prevent evasion, it was usually found necessary to support the provisions for common prices by rules about terms of payment, discounts and sometimes the packaging and delivery of goods. In the determination of these common prices the cartels used various methods. In some industries the arrangements were simple; in others very elaborate, at any rate in appearance. For the supply of cordage the Federation's accountants worked out the average costs of various types and grades of fibre over a period and then added a sum which measured the average cost of transport from the port to a number of representative manufacturers. To the sum so obtained a 'production factor' was applied, that is, a ratio indicative of the weight of fibre required to produce a given weight of cordage of a particular specification. To the raw material cost of a ton of each kind of cordage the accountant then added conversion costs, that is, the cost of production and sale which was in fact the weighted average of certain individual cost figures. After allowances for discounts or rebates, a profit margin determined separately for each section of the trade was added. The results were the recommended selling prices.[1] The different sections of the trade sometimes modified these recommendations by reference to other factors, including potential competition. In practice, it was seldom found possible to adopt the recommended prices without modification.

This procedure was fairly representative of that followed by many trades, although of course the nature of the product and the

[1] Monopolies and Restrictive Practices Commission, *Report on the Supply of Hard Fibre Cordage*, pp. 56 et seq.

market affected it in detail. Occasionally an effort was made to introduce a uniform system of costing so that the figures obtained from the various firms might be comparable. In some industries, as in linoleum, the costs supplied were worked out without any reference to a common method. In general, the relations between the average costs as determined by the accountants were by no means a decisive factor in pricing. The associations, it is true, began their discussions on prices with such costs before them, and with the knowledge of how those costs had changed in the recent past and how they were likely to move in the future. These data were certainly relevant to what they had to decide. Yet, when the prices were actually fixed, or when the proposed rate of profit for each product was decided on, the associations were always strongly influenced by what in their judgment the market would bear. It may be suspected that in many cases the elaborate cost-estimating procedure provided merely the façade behind which the price-making occurred. It lent an appearance of scientific respectability to what in the end turned out to be an estimate of market possibilities. The view is widely held that it is more virtuous to fix prices by relation to average costs than by relation to market conditions. Hence, even where the latter exert a determining influence, an effort is often made to disguise this fact by a pretence that costs are decisive.

In some of the industries examined by the Commission firms obtained their orders by tendering for contracts. The operation of restrictive practices in this field provided some curious examples of the monopolist's ingenuity. For example, in the London building industry members of the London Builders' Conference were required to report to the chairman their intention to tender whenever the work was likely to reach a certain value. Lists of the proposed tenderers were circulated among the competitors, and this information often led to decisions on the part of some of them to withdraw or to tender a 'cover price'.[1] For some contracts the

[1] A 'cover price' is a tender price sufficiently high to ensure that he who submits it does *not* win the contract.

Conference was accustomed to apply its Fair Price Scheme. Each competitor for a contract, before submitting his tender to the building owner, informed the Conference of his preliminary price, that is, the price that he initially proposed to tender. The chairman then reviewed the list of tenders. If any price seemed to him to be uneconomically low, he tried to persuade the tenderer to withdraw it or to modify it. After this adjustment had been made, the chairman then calculated the average of the lowest two-thirds of the tender prices and established this as the Fair Price for the job. The difference between the lowest original and the average was then, on the advice of the chairman, added to each of the tender prices before being submitted to the building owner. This additional sum was known as *Conad*. After the payment had been received by the successful tenderer on completion of the contract, the chairman divided the *Conad* among the various competitors. In some cases, where it was not considered necessary to add *Conad*, a sum representing the cost of tendering was added to each of the prices tendered and this sum (*Tenad*) was subsequently shared among the competitors.[1] Arrangements for adjusting tenders by mutual consultations among firms existed in other industries but few showed the degree of elaboration reached by the London builders.

The elimination or modification of price competition is, of course, the aim of most cartels, but price agreements alone are seldom sufficient to achieve it. Unless some joint control can be imposed over output or sales, the appearance of excessive capacity or output at the fixed level of prices is likely to disturb the loyalties of the member firms. So buttresses are devised in the form of quotas on sales or output, and of restrictions on freedom to operate plant or to make additions to capacity. One of the most interesting quotas schemes was introduced by the calico printing industry. Every participant in the scheme was allotted a 'percentage quantum' in the total money turnover of the trade. The allocation was based

[1] Monopolies and Restrictive Practices Commission, *Report on the Supply of Buildings in the Greater London Area*, Chapter 3.

on the distribution of output determined by the war-time scheme for the concentration of production. However, it was not rigid. Adjustments were made from year to year in accordance with a provision by which a member's quota was altered by the addition or subtraction of one-tenth of the difference between his quota for the previous year and the proportion of the total turnover which he actually achieved in that year. Quotas could be sold by one member to another under certain conditions. For exceeding his quota a member paid a sum equal to 20 per cent of the excess into a central fund. A member whose production fell short of his quota received a sum equal to 20 per cent of the deficiency.[1]

Arrangements for restricting capacity took several forms. In the manufacture of copper-semis, the cartel provided that special terms should be given to customers who undertook to limit their own capacity to manufacture products that could be supplied by members. In the calico printing trade, firms which sold their plants to others under the industry's redundancy scheme undertook not to re-enter the trade for a period. The leading firm in this industry itself made agreements with firms in other branches of textile finishing by which all undertook to limit the scope of their activities.[2] In the electric cables industry covenants existed which precluded some firms in allied trades from taking up the manufacture of cables.

Some of the investigations revealed that efforts were made to regulate imports. The British Match Corporation and the Swedish Match Corporation determined by agreement the shares of each firm in sales to the British market. The supply of canvas footwear and rubber boots from Hong Kong to the British market was covered by an agreement by which a group of British importers

[1] For a detailed description of this 'Percentage Quantum' scheme, see Monopolies and Restrictive Practices Commission, *Report on the Process of Calico Printing*, pp. 32–5. The cartel also laid down minimum prices for most of the production. The price lists issued were detailed and elaborate. There were also prescribed minimum charges for engraving rollers.

[2] ibid., pp. 35–6.

bought exclusively from a group of Hong Kong exporters. Membership of the two groups was restricted. In several branches of the electrical goods industry the associated firms operated a restrictive patent policy and controlled the supply of components or machinery with the object of penalizing outsiders. Some of them made use of fighting brands to meet the competition of non-associated firms in particular markets. For example, the Electric Lamp Manufacturers' Association produced cheap non-branded lamps which they sold in the low-priced stores in opposition to similar lamps produced by firms outside the Association.[1]

These then were the main restrictive practices disclosed by the Commission in the early years of its career. We now come to consider its judgments about the public interest, its suggestions for remedies where it found the practices contrary to the public interest and, finally, the reasons for its answers. In general, in its reports on individual industries, the Commission consistently condemned exclusive dealing arrangements, loyalty rebates, the collective enforcement of resale price maintenance, the rigging of tenders and, with minor exceptions, quota schemes. On price agreements its judgments were more variable. Thus, where it considered that a price agreement was necessary in order to preserve constructive co-operation in research or patent-sharing it was ready to tolerate the continuance of the agreement, provided that the prices fixed were reasonable, or that the cartel's arrangements for fixing the prices were satisfactory. This was the case with electric lamps. In the insulin industry the price-fixing arrangements were accepted partly on the ground that British insulin prices were low by international standards, and partly because the Ministry of Health, as a leading customer, was considered capable of exercising adequate countervailing power. Where these special circumstances did not exist, however, common price agreements were condemned, together with cognate discount agreements.

[1] Monopolies and Restrictive Practices Commission, *Report on the Supply of Electric Lamps*, p. 87.

Price agreements were considered to be particularly objectionable in industries where manufacturers' costs differed widely.

The remedy most commonly proposed was simply the abandonment of condemned practices, that is to say, the establishment of conditions for free competition. Generally this remedy was unqualified. Sometimes, however, the Commission was willing to allow an association to recommend prices to its members, provided that there was no question of their enforcement. In some industries it was clear that the mere abandonment of the condemned practices would fail to restore competition. In the electric cable industry, for instance, where the firms were few and the disposition to compete weak, it was evident that the elimination of the formal arrangement would make little difference to the way in which the business was conducted. In cases of this sort, the Commission often relied on countervailing power to maintain prices at a reasonable level. Where the purchaser was very large, this remedy might well be effective. Thus, in the cables industry the Commission called on the chief customers, namely the electricity supply authorities, to ensure that prices were satisfactory, and, in order to strengthen the customers' bargaining power, the Commission advised that they should be given access to the producer's costs. All customers were to have the right of sharing in these advantages. In some other industries it was recommended that monopolists should be required to cease to impose restrictions on the supply of components and special types of machinery to outside firms. For example, the Swedish Match Corporation, which controlled the chief supplier of match making machinery, had an agreement with the British Match Corporation to withhold the supply of machinery from the latter's competitors. This was condemned as being contrary to the public interest.[1] Occasionally firms, though active in support of common pricing arrangements, sought by devious methods (as by granting secret allowances to customers) to obtain additional business for themselves. The Commission, in

[1] Monopolies and Restrictive Practices Commission, *Report on the Supply and Export of Matches, etc.*, pp. 89–93.

its judgment on one such case in the tyre industry, came to the conclusion that competition, even in this clandestine form, was better than no competition at all.[1]

Having summarized the Commission's judgments on the main restrictive practices which it encountered in dealing with its references, we must now try to identify the principles which lay behind its judgments. As several commentators have already pointed out, the Commission paid little deference to welfare economics in reaching its conclusions. It is doubtful if it ever examined an industry's practice primarily from the standpoint of the allocation of resources. This may be partly because these principles would have seemed too abstract to the majority of the Commission, and partly because the economist members of the Commission, by the time of their appointment, had realized that welfare economics had little relevance to the practical questions before them. If the Commission were moved by any theoretical principles, it appears to have been those associated with Joseph Schumpeter, at any rate to the extent of agreeing with him that capacity to innovate and change was more important than the presence of pure or perfect competition. Consequently, practices that excited the disapprobation of the Committee were those which restricted entry to the trade, stereotyped the allocation of output among producers, and interfered with experiment in methods. In general, they took the view that the existence of free competition within the industry was the best method of achieving what was considered desirable, although the competition which they had in mind resembled 'workable' competition more closely than 'perfect' competition, which indeed was a theorist's toy and not a serious tool of economic policy.

The substitution of free or freer competition for restrictions was regarded as a means of securing an improved performance by an industry, and not as an end in itself. Where an industry appeared to have achieved a high level of performance, and showed alertness in the face of change, the Commission did not insist on the

[1] *Report on the Supply and Export of Pneumatic Tyres*, p. 126.

introduction of competitive conditions. This was so in the insulin case. Again, where price competition was incompatible with technical collaboration which the Commission might think to be highly conducive to rapid economic progress, as we have seen, limitations on price competition were permitted. It is significant that while the Commission always condemned the collective enforcement of RPM on the ground that this practice was detrimental to the freedom of firms to experiment with methods of distribution, it proposed the abolition of individual RPM only in exceptional cases. As long as an individual manufacturer had a choice in the way he disposed of his goods, as long as uniformity was not imposed on him, the Commission usually thought that there was no good reason for interfering with his choice.[1] Where the mere abolition of restrictions was unlikely to lead to keener competition in cases where this was considered desirable, the Commission fell back on the countervailing power of large customers to provide the safeguards and stimulus desired. This was sometimes a *pis aller*. The Commission had found in some industries that large buyers (e.g. the Post Office in its purchase of cables) did not always exert themselves to get better terms from the suppliers. Thus, the procurement officers of government departments sometimes found that life was easier for them if they were on good terms with the manufacturers rather than if they were keen purchasers. The Commission rarely advocated official price control as a means of maintaining a satisfactory level of prices.[2] It knew that the Government had dismantled its wartime price control machinery and would almost certainly hesitate to re-establish it. Furthermore, the few members of the Commission who had had experience of price control in the early post-war period were sceptical of its effectiveness in peace-time. The Commission has been criticized for failing to probe deeply into the operating efficiency of the firms under examination. But it was not designed for that task. It rightly

[1] See Chapter VIII for further discussion of this question.

[2] However, price control was recommended for the match industry and for industrial and medical gases.

directed its attention to the more limited objective of eliminating certain kinds of practice that were detrimental to efficiency and of calling into being market conditions conducive to economic progress.

So far we have been concerned with the Commission's work in investigating particular industries. Yet, the most important of the Commission's reports, important because of the subsequent part it played in the evolution of policy, was its general report on Collective Discrimination. The reference of which this report was the outcome differed from all the others in that it called for an investigation of certain restrictions generally practised. The inquiry, that is to say, was not limited to particular goods or industries. This type of reference was covered by Clause 15 of the 1948 Act, which empowered the Board of Trade to require the Commission to report 'on the general effect in the public interest of practices of a specified class', provided that these practices had been dealt with in previous reports. Now, as we have seen, certain practices affecting the relations of manufacturers and distributors were found by the Commission to be prevalent in most of the industries investigated. These included exclusive dealing and other discriminatory trade practices. They were identified and classified by the Commission as follows:[1]

1 Collective discrimination by sellers without any corresponding obligation on the buyers.
2 Collective discrimination by sellers in return for exclusive buying obligations.
3 Collective adoption by sellers of a policy of maintaining resale prices or imposing other trading obligations on buyers.
4 Collective discrimination by sellers to enforce resale prices.
5 Collective discrimination by buyers without obligations on the part of sellers.
6 Aggregated rebates.

Some of these practices had already been considered by other

[1] *Report on Collective Discrimination*, pp. 11–12.

investigators, as by the Committee on Resale Maintenance which reported in 1949. Thus, the ground was well prepared. The Commission, for its part, drew on the evidence collected in its previous investigations as well as on the results of enquiries undertaken specifically for the purpose of this reference. The findings were consistent with the Commission's judgments on the effect of the practices in particular industries. The majority of members held that all the practices were contrary to the public interest and that only in exceptional cases could justification be found for retaining them. The restrictions frustrated those firms who wished to innovate, or who wished to experiment with methods of distribution. The objection to the practices because they created 'undue rigidity' was indeed fundamental. The activities of the private courts instituted for trying offenders against the rules of the associations were considered odious. It was admitted that there might be circumstances in which free competition did not provide all the safeguards necessary for the public interest, but where this was so, the State or an independent authority should normally take the responsibility for permitting any kind of restriction.

The majority of the Commission proposed that there should be legislation to prohibit the condemned practices, with provision for granting exemptions in special cases. A minority were in favour simply of registering the practices and examining them case by case. The report on Collective Discrimination can be regarded as epitomizing the work of the Commission and the operation of the monopoly policy in its first phase. If it revealed rather deeper divisions among the members of the Commission than the previous reports, this was only to be expected. Such a body is more likely to reach agreement in particular cases than to accept broad principles or rules applicable to the economy as a whole or to large categories of transactions. Moreover, in the general reference, as in others, the disagreement turned less on the effect of restrictive practices on the public interest than on the remedies judged to be expedient in the particular circumstances.

At this point it may be useful to review the arguments put

forward by the associations and firms to justify their practices, for these throw light on the attitude of British industry to the policy as a whole. It must be emphasized that the majority of British industrialists and their representatives who appeared before the Commission in the ten years after its establishment had gained their early business experience during the period of depression before the Second World War. Their minds had been deeply affected by the conditions of that time when prices and profits were under severe pressure and when there was little inducement or ability to make cost-saving investments. As we have already seen, the governments of the 1930s, far from being hostile to cartels, had actively encouraged them and in some industries had obliged firms to introduce measures for eliminating competition. During the Second World War the market as a regulator of economic processes had been virtually destroyed, and even firms which were not engaged on government contracts operated in an environment of price and production controls and rationing. In the latter part of the war, discussions between government and industry about reconstruction turned largely on questions of the collaboration between the member firms of an industry, and the relations between the Government and representative bodies of businessmen, rather than on the restoration of a free market. The Working Parties set up by the Board of Trade just after the war to examine the policy of a number of industries usually reported in favour of establishing for every industry a representative body armed with powers of levying its members for the purposes of financing joint activities. Development Councils were formed in a few industries in accordance with these recommendations. On the whole, the civil servants with whom industrialists discussed these matters also inherited pre-war attitudes towards competition and restrictive practices.

It is natural, therefore, that the businessmen who appeared before the Commission, at any rate in the early days, expressed surprise and indignation that their practices should be scrutinized, let alone condemned as pernicious. 'Why,' asked typical witnesses before the Commission, 'should a firm or group of firms be adversely criticized for practices which were common to a great part of industry and had been actively encouraged by the Government a short time ago?' Most firms strongly resented the imputation that what they were doing was contrary to the public interest. When it came to the positive defence of the practices, the arguments differed little from one industry to another. Unless a firm enjoyed reasonable security from 'unfair competition' it was unlikely to invest in research and development and in cost reducing equipment, or to maintain a sufficiently constant throughput to achieve economies of scale. A firm exposed to ruthless competition was under the temptation to reduce quality in its efforts to cut its costs, and it would be unable to provide the service of the kind needed by its customers. Sometimes restrictive practices were necessary to save customers from the consequences of their own stupidity. For instance, in the electric lamp cartel there was a rule whereby member firms were penalized if they produced lamps with a life of more than 1,500 hours. This restriction was justified on the ground that after 1,500 hours of life the luminous efficiency of a lamp declined and its continued use after that period was uneconomic.[1] The user, it was alleged, was not likely to be aware of this.

Restrictions imposed on distributive channels were often defended on the ground that it was both the interest and the duty of the manufacturers (individually or as a trade) to ensure that competent dealers handled their goods. Collective arrangements for the enforcement of RPM were said to be the only way available to many firms for ensuring that there was a sufficient number of competent distributors to meet the public's convenience. It was also claimed that price stability was invariably beneficial to producer and consumer alike and that concerted measures were needed to maintain that stability. Many of the associations agreed that the regulation of competition might in theory result in prices being too high, but they were unanimous in denying that the prices fixed by them

[1] *Report on the Supply of Electric Lamps*, pp. 45–6, 97–8.

were open to that criticism. Some declared that, without regulation, prices would be likely to rise in the short run because free competition would increase risks and in the long run because it would discourage the long-range planning of production and cost-reducing investment.

All these arguments related to restrictive practices, that is the 'things done' by the firms and not to the fact of market dominance. In the period from 1948 to 1956 the Commission seldom had to consider problems concerned with monopolies of scale. These problems, which became its major interest after 1956, will be discussed later. But it is worth noting here that the British Match Corporation argued that the essence of the public interest 'is believed to lie in the policy of an industry as distinguished from its structure'.[1] This proposition seems to have been accepted by the Commission which confined its strictures to those practices of monopolists which were designed to establish or preserve their market power.[2]

In all its enquiries the Commission undertook a scrutiny of costs, prices and profits. Some of these investigations were elaborate. They were designed to reveal for the industry as a whole, or for particular firms, the costs, distributive margins, levels of actual prices (compared with minimum prices fixed by agreement) and the profit on capital employed for a recent period. The meaning and the identification of 'capital employed' gave rise to disputes between the Commission's accountants and those of industry, and when these were not resolved the alternative rates of profit were often shown in the report. It was usual for the Commission to compare the rates of profit earned in the industries investigated with those in industry as a whole or some sections of it.

Although this part of the enquiry contributed to a proper understanding of how the industry conducted its affairs, it exerted only

[1] *Report on the Supply and Export of Matches, etc.*, p. 78.

[2] See Chapter IX for further discussion of policy towards monopolies of scale.

a modest influence over the findings and recommendations of the Commission. It is true that where the investigation revealed a wide spread of costs among the firms, the Commission's objections to common prices or market sharing were strengthened. But it is difficult to deny that the cost and price investigations became something of a ritual in the Commission's procedure and that the bearing of the facts disclosed by them on its conclusions was not always easy to understand. This criticism had less force where the Commission was dealing with a single firm monopoly than where it was concerned with a cartel, but it is probable that the cost, price and profit enquiries reinforced rather than determined conclusions that had been reached for other reasons. Apart from the technical difficulty of determining the costs of a particular product in a multi-product firm, or of obtaining comparable cost figures from a group of firms, or of measuring capital employed, there remains the problem of deciding in a particular case whether, in the absence of a free market, the prices or the rate of profit are 'reasonable'. The Commission recognized that where risks were exceptionally high, firms were justified in aiming at a high rate of profit, but again, in the absence of a free market, to determine just what level of profit is right in a particular case is a matter for arbitrary judgment. It must be remembered that the law did not proclaim that monopoly itself was contrary to the public interest; the relevant considerations were the way the monopolist used his power and his performance. As to cartels, the Commission usually found sufficient evidence for their conclusions in the restrictive practices themselves and their effects. Wherever an approximation to a free competitive market could be reached by the abolition of the restrictions, then it was otiose to take a decision about performance based on the record of prices, cost and profits.

Finally, we must say a word about the results of the Commission's work. The Government formally accepted the majority of the recommendations, but it was inactive in applying them. In only one case before 1956 (the first) was an Order made under the Act to enforce the decisions.[1] For the rest the Government preferred to obtain the 'voluntary' agreement of the industry to abandon the condemned practices. This process, which required a series of meetings between the Board of Trade and the industry, usually took a year or eighteen months, and frequently the outcome was a compromise between the Commission's accepted recommendations and the industry's preferences. The Government obviously had no intention at this time of pursuing a vigorous anti-monopoly policy.

Nevertheless, the proceedings and the reports of the Commission exerted a powerful influence on the attitude to restrictive practices both in board-rooms and in the market place. The reports received wide publicity, and it was not agreeable for industries or particular firms to see their business methods revealed and condemned. Politicians, journalists and the general public became more closely acquainted with the activities of cartels and monoplies and with the informed criticisms directed at them. The former complacency was disturbed. The main achievement, therefore, was the creation of opinion critical of restrictive practices. Even firms which were not brought under scrutiny took notice of the Commission's conclusions and sometimes modified their practices accordingly. In the later enquiries, for example, it was found that some cartels, by the time they were brought before the Commission, had abandoned former practices of the kind which a reading of the Commission's reports showed were liable to be condemned. It cannot be claimed that the Commission did much to infuse a vigorous competitive spirit into British industry, but at least its work opened the way for the next step forward. The principles which informed the Restrictive Trade Practices Act of 1956 were derived largely from the experiences of the Monopolies Commission without whose preparatory work the new legislation would never have commended itself to Parliament and the country.

[1] Even this Order had to be quickly withdrawn because of deficiencies in its drafting.

CHAPTER VII

The Restrictive Practices Court

By 1955 the time had come for another stage in the evolution of monopoly policy. It was then confidently expected that the Government, while retaining the existing procedure for enquiry and report, would introduce legislation to prohibit certain practices adversely reported on and would possibly lay down criteria to guide the Commission in its future judgments of the public interest. In fact, the policy took a different direction. Although by this time most businessmen were agreed, in general principle, that where monopoly existed the State could not remain indifferent to its potential dangers, they were strongly critical of the procedure introduced by the Act of 1948. This criticism arose in part out of the piecemeal approach which that legislation prescribed. The selection of an industry for investigation was, of necessity, rather arbitrary, and this itself produced resentment among the firms under scrutiny. The resentment was caused not only because of the trouble and expense involved but also because an industry brought before the Commission felt itself to be on trial. There were, of course, no logical grounds for such an attitude. There was no enactment that condemned monopoly or restrictive practices as such. The Commission was charged simply with discovering the economic effects of an industry's practices and, in the light of the evidence, with indicating what action should be taken to remedy any ill effects. Until the Government had accepted the recommendations there was no question of attaching blame to an industry.

Yet explanations of this sort failed to disturb the conviction of the industrialists who were being investigated that they were being pilloried for activities which no law condemned. The complaint was made that the Commission acted both as prosecutor and judge, and the reply that the Commission was not engaged in prosecuting offenders but rather in finding out what the law on certain practices ought to be was unconvincing. It was claimed that, despite the 'public interest' hearings, the Commission failed to give the industry concerned a clear indication of the practices that it regarded as reprehensible and of its reasons for that view. The industry, after the Commission had reached its final conclusion, was afforded no opportunity of defending itself against any charges until the report had reached the Board of Trade. While subsequent discussions with that Department might affect policy on the matters reported to it, the report was in fact published in the form sent forward by the Commission. For all these reasons, if the monopoly policy was to be carried further, the business world favoured a judicial procedure, because then the nature of an alleged offence would be precisely defined.

The strength of this opinion persuaded the Government to go far towards abandoning the administrative procedure followed up to that time, and to bring in legislation which gave to the business world the alternative it favoured. When the industrialists expressed their preferences, however, they did not foresee that the Act would provide for a new and vigorous attack on restrictive practices. If they had known that this was the alternative to the existing procedure, their views might have been different. The Government itself yielded easily to industrial pressure because once the new procedure had been introduced, the onus of taking decisions in particular cases was transferred to the Courts. Ministers were not reluctant to relieve themselves of their responsibilities. They had made obeisance to the anti-monopoly principle and now they could pass to others the job of executing the policy.

The structure of the Act can be briefly described. It fell into three parts. Part II prohibited collective arrangements for enforcing resale price maintenance and at the same time increased the power of individual suppliers to enforce their resale prices through the Courts. Part III of the Act reconstituted the Monopolies Commission with reduced responsibilities. These two Parts will be considered in subsequent chapters, and we shall here deal with Part I. Under its provisions restrictive practices of a type defined had to be registered and their contents set out in detail.[1] The practices included price agreements at all levels, exclusive dealing arrangements, loyalty rebates, aggregated rebates, agreement on credit terms, quotas on output or sales, restrictions on capacity and market sharing. The arrangements to be registered covered those between manufacturer and customer as well as those between firms in the same stage of industry. The most important exclusions consisted of services and trade union activities together with certain official marketing schemes and other restrictive arrangements sponsored by the Government.

The Act established a new Court, the Restrictive Practices Court, with the function of adjudicating on cases brought before it by the Registrar of Restrictive Trade Practices. This person was a new administrative officer who held a key position in carrying out the policy. He was responsible not only for the registration of agreements but also for initiating proceedings. The Court itself was composed both of High Court judges and also of lay members who were persons 'qualified by virtue of knowledge of or experience in industry, commerce, or public affairs'.

The passing of this Act brought a striking change in policy as well as procedure. The law had now ceased to be neutral in respect of certain restrictive practices and had become definitely hostile. In other words, the Act contained a presumption that those prac-

[1] Although there is an obligation on the parties to register agreements, failure to do so is no crime. Even if the non-registered agreement is discovered, and if the failure to register is proved to have been wilful, the most that can happen is that it may be declared contrary to the public interest and so void. Thus, some agreements of a restrictive character were not registered, and not all of these have been discovered by the Registrar. Cf. R. B. Stevens and B. S. Yamey, *The Restrictive Practices Court*, p. 159.

tices were against the public interest and should be prohibited. The onus was now placed on persons who wished to continue the restrictions to show that the proscription was unjustified in particular instances. They could attempt to do this by convincing the Court that they had satisfied certain conditions laid down in Section 21 of the Act. These are the seven so-called 'gateways' or 'escape routes'. They are shown *in extenso* in the Appendix.[1] It will be observed that the circumstances which might be held to justify the retention of restrictive practices varied widely. Thus, an agreement might continue if its removal would cause consumers to lose a specific and substantial benefit, or if it protected the public against injury, or if it was an offset to the restrictive practices of an association, or if it was required to enable the producers to deal with a monopoly buyer or customer, or if it adversely affected employment or exports. A firm, however, might succeed in getting through one of these 'gateways' and yet fail to win its case. For there is a 'tail-piece' in Section 21 which required the Court to be satisfied that the advantages of allowing the agreement to continue, by reason of one or more of the 'gateways', were not balanced by any detriment to the public interest. Such a balancing judgment demanded economic insight of a high order from the members of the Court.

From the terms of the Act it appeared that few cartels or restrictive practices were likely to survive. The early decisions of the Court bore out this opinion, for while they did not depend on a presumption that competition was necessarily beneficial to the public interest,[2] they showed its scepticism about submissions that the restrictions imposed on competition in these cases were a social advantage. It is not our purpose to review the decisions in detail, but a few examples may throw light on the Court's operations. The first decision concerned the Chemists' Federation Agreement. This agreement provided, *inter alia*, for the restriction of the sale of

[1] See pp. 169–70.

[2] In this respect the law in the United Kingdom is still far removed from that of the United States, see Chapter X.

proprietory medicines to licensed chemists' shops. It was defended mainly on the ground that the abandonment of the restriction would open up dangers to the health of the public. The Court rejected this argument partly because no convincing evidence of the danger had been produced, and partly because the control exercised by the Federation was in any case insufficient to furnish any safeguard. In the next case, the Yarn Spinners' Association defended its minimum price agreements chiefly on the ground that their abandonment would reduce employment in Lancashire. The Court accepted this argument, but at the same time found that the agreement had the effect of raising prices, diminishing exports, and creating excessive capacity in the industry. These detriments were considered to outweigh the benefits, and the agreement had to go. In this and other cases brought before it the Court expressed its scepticism about the advantages of price stability when this was attained by sacrificing free competition, and it invariably rejected the oft-repeated argument, which had been frequently heard by the Monopolies Commission, that price competition was likely to debase quality.

The early decisions suggested that very few restrictive agreements were likely to survive. In the first two-and-a-half years of the Court's work, from November 1958 to March 1961, in only two out of thirteen contested cases were the restrictions upheld. In one case (Water Tube Boilers) the successful defence depended mainly on the alleged advantages of collusive tendering to the export trade, and in the other case (Black Bolts and Nuts) the Association succeeded because the price agreements were supposed to save customers from the tedium of 'shopping around'. In the first of these two cases the economic grounds for the decisions are sound enough, since the public interest with which the law is concerned is that of the inhabitants of the United Kingdom and not that of mankind at large. The second decision is regarded by economists as an aberration of judgment similar to that which occasionally causes weary examiners to award high marks to a mediocre script. The argument which the Court found convincing for the bolts and nuts industry has been put forward in defence of other agreements without success.

In March 1961 there seems to have been a change of direction, for the Court gave a decision which promised cartels a new lease of life. This was in the Cement case. The Cement Makers' Federation operated an agreement for common delivered prices which, of course, involved the subsidization of buyers remote from any cement works at the expense of nearby buyers. The main argument used to support this practice was that the agreement, by eliminating price competition, reduced the risks of the firms and so the return on capital required by them. The Court accepted the argument about risk as self-evident, although strong arguments to the contrary could have been put forward, and it reached the conclusion not only that the agreement kept the price lower than it would have been under free competition, but also that even the nearby buyers who were discriminated against were better off under the existing arrangement. It was consistent with the Court's findings that it should have concluded that the industry had operated at a lower average rate of profit on capital employed than manufacturing industries in general. Indeed, the conclusion that the cartelized industry had earned only a 'reasonable' rate of profit was a powerful argument in its defence.

Both the facts in regard to profits and the reasoning that convinced the Court have been challenged by critics.[1] The delivered pricing system which disregards the relationship between prices and the costs to individual works of supplying customers in different areas is likely to lead to a misallocation of resources and is prima facie mischievous. The Court seems to have doubted whether, even in the absence of the arrangement, market forces would have brought any closer approximation between prices and the costs of individual works. This doubt was based on the fact that the industry was dominated by the largest firm which was the natural price leader. The Court probably underestimated the extent to

[1] Notably by A. Sutherland, 'Economics in the Restrictive Practices Court' in *Oxford Economic Papers*, vol. 17, no. 3, November 1965.

which price leadership is vulnerable if it is not supported by cartel agreements. But it did not regard itself as properly concerned with structural problems or with alternative ways of organizing the industry so as to improve its performance. It limited its attention to the effect of a particular agreement within an existing structure.

The Court also upheld the system of agreed delivered prices for glazed and floor tiles. It was persuaded that the abrogation of the agreement would destroy the standardization of products which was believed to be a source of economy and that prices would consequently be raised. It rejected the argument of the Registrar that, given free competition, there would be a tendency for each producer to specialize on those tiles which he could make most cheaply, and that this specialization was more likely to lead to low costs and prices than the standardization policy of the cartel. A decision favourable to the associated producers was reached, for much the same reason, in the case of steel scrap.

Economists have been inclined to regard with much disfavour the decision reached in the Permanent Magnets case. The price agreement in this industry was upheld by the Court on the ground that the prices charged were reasonable, for they resulted in no more than an adequate return on the capital employed in an industry which was efficiently run. A decision based on a view of the industry's efficiency (a fact which is exceedingly difficult for an outsider to determine with any certainty) is always open to criticism. The very concept of an efficiently run *industry*, when this is composed of several firms, is nebulous. It is improbable that all firms are equally efficient; and only if there is competition among them can their relative efficiency be demonstrated. The Court, however, was also influenced by the fact that the members of the industry had co-operated technically with one another, with benefit to themselves and their customers, and it considered that if price competition were introduced the technical co-operation might cease. We have noted that a similar argument has been accepted by the Monopolies Commission in the electric lamp enquiry.

One of the most interesting cases in which the Court upheld a restrictive practice was that of the Net Book Agreement. This agreement, the origins of which go back to the last decade of the nineteenth century, turned on a system by which individual publishers made contracts with booksellers to maintain the resale price of their books. There was no compulsion on the publisher to prescribe a retail price for any book, but in fact for the vast majority of books published the retail price *was* fixed. The Court accepted the argument that unrestricted competition among retailers, while lowering the price of popular books, would reduce the net revenue of the stock-holding booksellers on whom publishers rely for the sale of serious, slow-moving books. As a result, the number of those booksellers would decline and the number of titles in the more serious class of book would diminish. It was likely, moreover, that their prices would rise, because publishers would have to offer higher gross margins to the stock-holding booksellers. As the reading public would then lose 'specific and substantial benefits', the Court decided that the agreement should continue. The apparently sophisticated economic reasoning behind this decision has been subjected to harsh criticism.[1] The decision itself may nevertheless be defensible, if not for economic reasons, by reference to the (undemocratic) proposition that it is fitting that the reader of popular books should subsidize the student and the scholar.[2]

It is evident that after the Cement Federation case the destruction of the cartels was somewhat less vigorously pursued than in the earlier years of the Court's existence. Nevertheless, in the majority of cases the agreements were condemned. The question to which we must consequently address ourselves concerns the general effect of the decisions on industrial organization and business conduct. Formally, the effect on the cartels has been

[1] R. B. Stevens and B. S. Yamey, *The Restrictive Practices Court*, pp. 224–35; A. Sutherland, loc. cit., p. 398–9 and 'Are Books Different?' in *The Solicitor Quarterly*, October, 1963, pp. 323–38. For a contrary view, see P. W. S. Andrews, 'In Mr Sutherland's Bad Books' in *The Solicitor Quarterly*, January, 1964.

[2] Cf. T. Wilson, 'Restrictive Practices' in J. P. Miller, *Competition, Cartels and Their Regulation.*

devastating. Apart from the agreements which were abandoned between the time of the passing of the Act and the date for compulsory registration, large numbers of agreements were cancelled after registration by a voluntary act of the firms or in the prompting of the Registrar. Some were amended so as to remove their restrictive clauses. Others were de-registered because they were judged by the Registrar to have no economic significance. The agreements removed from the Register in these ways far exceeded in number those which were given up as the result of an unfavourable Court decision. By June 1963, 1,610 out of 2,430 registered agreements had been 'terminated by act of the parties or effluxion of time or from which all registrable restrictions had been removed by virtue of an Order of the Court or by an act of the parties'.[1] It is probable that many of the remainder have been, or will be, abrogated on receiving from the Registrar notice of proceedings against them. Despite the tendency of the Court to take a rather more favourable view than originally of certain types of restrictive practices, cartels have certainly remained very vulnerable.

The change in the status of cartels, however, has not obviously lifted British industry to a new plane of efficiency, nor has it transformed the market conditions under which the majority of firms have operated. Of course, no informed observer of the industrial scene would have expected such revolutionary results. An economist who in 1961 published a report of his investigations into the consequences of the abandonment of agreements estimated that up to June 1959 competition had increased, and prices had been reduced, in about a third of the cases examined.[2] This is a substantial result, since it may be presumed that some of the now abandoned cartels had exerted little influence on prices or competition. In some industries, however, the effect on competition was short-lived and the firms found alternative routes to restric-

[1] Registrar of Restrictive Trading Agreements, *Report for the Period July 1, 1961, to June 30, 1963*, p. 10.

[2] J. B. Heath, 'Restrictive Practices and After', in *Manchester School*, Vol. XXIX, No. 2 (May 1961).

tion. An example frequently quoted is that of the electric cables industry. There the abrogation of the price agreements led immediately to keen competition and to steep price reductions. But this was followed by a series of amalgamations and the emergence of the largest firm as the price leader. Whether the new structure is technically or commercially more efficient than the old is uncertain. It is clear, however, that the market for cables was highly competitive for a very brief period only.

The establishment of price leadership seems to have become a quite usual response to the breakdown of formal cartel arrangements. In addition, firms discovered other means for mitigating the severities of unwelcome competition. The most common of these has been the 'open price agreement' or 'information agreement'. According to this, firms undertake to notify each other, through their trade association, about such matters as prices, distributive margins, conditions of sale, costs, orders and output. The information is circulated throughout the trade and, although no recommendation accompanies the figures, the hope and expectation are that the behaviour of the firms will be affected by this knowledge of what others are doing. In industries where orders are obtained by tender, firms may agree to notify their associations of their prices quoted after the tender has been submitted (or the contract let) and these bids are distributed to all members of the trade. Most types of cartel restrictions have their counterparts in informal arrangements. Minimum price agreements are paralleled by the exchange of actual prices, quota schemes by the notification of turnover, contract allocation by 'bid filing', and collective RPM by an exchange of list prices. A distinction may be drawn between information agreements that relate to intentions and those that relate to actions already taken by firms. Obviously it is the former that are likely to exert the strongest influence on future conduct.

The view that these agreements, though they might be intended to have the same effect as the prohibited practices, were not normally registrable was accepted by the Registrar. After the Austin judgment it seemed probable that the Court would take the same view in cases where bilateral restrictive contracts had been substituted for multilateral contracts.[1] This probability, however, was disturbed by a decision in the British Basic Slag case.[2] The Registrar also, to judge from statements in his report for 1963, had by then become more hopeful that some of the 'information' agreements might be registrable. A proposal to remove the doubt was made in a White Paper issued in the spring of 1964 which called for the registration of information agreements. The monopoly legislation of the Government that took office in the autumn of that year has so far been silent on this question.[3] Consequently, those who hoped to close this loophole must still rely in the Court's willingness to maintain the broader interpretation of the 1956 Act which was given in the Basic Slag case.

An example of the ingenuity shown by industrialists in finding substitutes for condemned practices is provided by the experience of the Monopolies Commission in its investigation into the trade in imported timber. This is of particular interest because the alternative devices, adopted by the trade after its original restrictions had been withdrawn, have been subjected to detailed scrutiny. Briefly the facts are these. The trade in imported timber involved the co-operation of a variety of dealers, each with specific functions, and

[1] The Austin Motor Company had re-drafted many of its restrictive agreements with its distributors in order to avoid registration. It did this by making bipartite agreements between itself and each of its distributors in regard to resale prices and other matters. The Court accepted the Registrar's contention that these agreements had the same effect as those which they replaced, but it decided that this did not make the agreement registrable. The Court, in other words, preferred a strictly literal interpretation of the words of the Act and seemed unconcerned with its intention.

[2] A number of steel companies agreed *individually* to sell their basic slag to a marketing company, British Basic Slag Limited, the board of which included steel company directors. The Court held that the arrangements were registrable because, although they were all made individually, they were mutually dependent in the sense that communications among the firms had aroused the expectation that each of them would act in the same way.

[3] See Chapter IX for a discussion of this White Paper and the Act of 1965.

the structure of the trade had developed so as to allow for the discharge of these functions. The agent in Britain of the foreign shipper normally sold the timber to an importer who in turn sold it to a merchant from whom most users obtained their supplies. In each section of the trade (hardwood, softwood and plywood) it was agreed that this channelling of supplies should be rigidly adhered to by all members of the trade and the terms of the transactions at each stage were controlled. This meant that a large user (say, a furniture manufacturer) with considerable expertise in the commodity was obliged to obtain his supplies from a merchant in the same way as a small user, even though he might have made substantial economies by going direct to the importer or even the shipper's agent. The Monopolies Commission condemned these restrictions, and the associations which administered them accepted the Board of Trade's proposal that they should be abandoned. For a time there was free competition. Soon, however, the larger users again found that they were being refused supplies except through the 'normal' channels. A further investigation brought to light that, although the formal agreements had not been revived, the trade associations were advising their members to maintain the 'structure of prices' and to adhere to trading practices similar to those of the former cartel. In other words, tacit arrangements had been substituted for the enforced restrictions which the associations had agreed to abandon, and 'as regards both hardwood and softwood the effects of the arrangements [were] similar to the effects of the former agreements and undertakings'.[1] The Commission condemned the new arrangements, and the Board of Trade laid an Order before Parliament in order to carry out the Commission's recommendations.

It is clearly not easy to oblige businessmen to compete if they object to doing so. Those brought up in an environment where restrictive practices were the rule are likely to be more actively

[1] Monopolies Commission, *Imported Timber: Report on whether and to what extent the Recommendation of the Commission has been complied with*, p. 57. This finding did not apply to plywood.

concerned with circumventing the intentions of the law than in co-operating in its application. This is especially so when they remain unconvinced that free competition is in the public interest, just as they are sure that it is contrary to their own. Yet, the results that have so far been achieved by the anti-monopoly policy in Great Britain should not be underestimated. As already emphasized, that policy has been applied to a generation of businessmen to whom cartels and restrictive agreements seemed normal and necessary. These have suffered a salutary shock which has led many of them to re-appraise their methods of conducting business. If free and vigorous competition is still by no means widespread in Great Britain, it can at least be said that there has occurred some 'loosening up' of formerly rigid industrial structures and conventional business behaviour. The Registrar himself has taken a more favourable view of the results as time has gone on. Thus, in his second Report, published in 1961, he had stated that the ending of agreements had not apparently been followed by widespread price reductions largely because of the 'forces of inertia'. In his third Report, however, issued in 1963, he observed that some industries formerly governed by restrictions were now keenly competitive. In other industries where the distributed price lists remained unchanged, large buyers found that in practice they could obtain special discounts more easily than in the past. This, he thought, was a hopeful sign, for it was to be expected that the stimulus to competition after a long period of price uniformity was most likely to come from the large buyers. A commentator on the policy has remarked: '[The Registrar] seemed disposed to place considerable reliance on countervailing power as an instrument for breaking down the established restrictive framework.'[1] At the same time the Registrar seemed less sanguine about the effects of the policy on competition in the distributive trades, but since then the law on resale price maintenance has been transformed. This will now be considered.

[1] A. Hunter, *Competition and the Law*, p. 185.

CHAPTER VIII

Resale Price Maintenance

Competition in the retail trade is generally imperfect, partly because of customer-goodwill and partly because the geographical distribution of the shops leads to a fragmentation of the market. Retailers even in the same line of business, follow different trading policies which are not always closely related to the market opportunities available to them. There are variations among them in the range of articles supplied, the rate of stock-turn and the services or amenities offered to customers. Since what is provided is differentiated, even when the physical product is identical, it might be expected that prices for the same article would differ widely from shop to shop. In fact, what is most striking is the similarity or identity of prices for the same physical product. Since the costs of distribution vary so greatly from shop to shop, the similarity or identity is further evidence of the extreme imperfection of the market. The imperfection is also demonstrated by the practice of the customary 'mark-up', that is, the addition (which varies from trade to trade) made by the retailer to his buying prices. During the last half-century the constraints on competition have been much increased by the introduction of resale price maintenance, that is, the stipulation by a supplier that his distributors (wholesalers or retailers) shall re-sell particular goods at prices fixed by him, or for not less than those prices.

The goods to which the practice applies are branded or proprietory goods which are often extensively advertised by the manufacturer. Most of them are consumer goods, although not all consumer goods have been equally affected by the spread of the practice. Cigarettes, confectionery, cereals, motor-cars, electrical goods, books, newspapers, chemists' goods are nearly all price maintained. On the other hand, foodstuffs (other than packaged foodstuffs) and household textiles have not been much affected. It has been estimated that in recent years about a quarter of all personal consumer expenditure in Great Britain has been spent on price-maintained goods.[1]

As with many monopolistic practices, the origins of RPM can be traced to the efforts of established producers to protect themselves against the competition of innovators, notably the multiples, which began to become important in the later years of the nineteenth century. Whereas the traditional specialist shopkeepers provided lavish service and credit and operated with high gross margins, the multiples gave little service and sought their profits by following a policy of low margins and high turnover. Small shopkeepers and stall-holders in especially favourable locations often followed the same policy. The development of multiples occurred at a time when manufacturers were introducing branded articles on a considerable scale. The sale of these depended heavily on consumer goodwill. So the traditional retailer saw an opportunity of bringing pressure to bear on the manufacturers with the object of checking the competition from their rivals. They formed associations and urged the manufacturers to adopt a policy of resale price maintenance for branded articles. At first, most of the manufacturers were hostile or indifferent to the practice, but in many trades they felt obliged to yield to the importunities of the retailers. Even if a particular manufacturer disapproved of RPM, it was difficult for him to refuse to fall in line with the policy of his competitors. As the manufacturers became accustomed to the practice, they themselves tended to become apologists for the system. Once it had become firmly established in a trade they were likely to defend it vigorously against criticism, for each of them

[1] B. S. Yamey, *Resale Price Maintenance* (Hobart Paper, Fourth Edition), p. 8.

feared the effect of its abandonment on his own business. Some large distributing firms which built up their trade by price-cutting before RPM had become strictly enforced turned into powerful supporters of the practice, once they were well established.

The restrictions imposed varied with the types of goods sold. For goods subject to 'impulse buying', the manufacturer wished to ensure that his products were available at numerous distributing points. If he practised RPM, therefore, he had to fix a large distributive margin so as to induce high-cost retailers to stock his goods. At these margins the retailer who, because of an exceptionally favourable location, operated with low costs, was likely to earn a high net revenue, and he came under a strong temptation to cut his prices, especially if the market confronting him was very elastic. The manufacturer had to ensure that the low-cost retailer resisted this temptation, as otherwise his goodwill with the other retailers would suffer. Tobacco and confectionery are examples of goods in this class.

Where a manufacturer was selling a consumer durable goods which required pre-sales or post-sales service (e.g. domestic electrical apparatus) he would be interested in seeing that his distributors were competent to render that service. So he was likely to restrict the number of dealers engaged in handling his goods and to fix margins adequate to ensure that they could cover the costs involved. Manufacturers of this class of goods were particularly vulnerable to the pressure of organized distributors. If it was found that some of the goods were being sold by traders at less than list prices, the rest of the traders could either use their influence to divert their customers' interest to rival products, or reduce the services provided by them on the now less profitable lines.

In order to enforce his resale prices, the manufacturer might make price a condition of sale in his contract with the retail customer, and this could be enforced in the Courts. Before 1956 the legal position was complicated where a wholesaler intervened between a manufacturer and a retailer, as was the case with most classes of consumer goods. Then the manufacturer's contract was solely with the wholesaler, and he had no remedy against price-cutting retailers, unless the article was patented. The manufacturer could, of course, persuade his wholesalers to withhold supplies from an offender, but in industries where there were numerous wholesalers this was often not an effective sanction. So the most usual method of enforcement was through collective arrangements administered by trade associations. A manufacturer-member would inform the secretary of the association about the resale prices fixed for his goods, and the association would assume the responsibility of seeing that these were adhered to. A dealer found to be cutting prices would probably be warned on the occasion of his first offence. If he persisted, his name would be placed on a Stop List and all the members of the trade, both manufacturers and wholesalers, would be instructed to withhold supplies from him. For example, the Proprietary Articles Trade Association, by a decision to boycott a retail chemist, could deprive him of supplies of all goods subject to RPM that fell within the Association's province. This action would probably put him out of business. A few trade associations set up private courts to try offenders and to impose penalties. Some of these courts were presided over by independent chairmen with legal experience and they followed formal rules of procedure. The application of sanctions by trade associations was contested in the Courts during the inter-war years, but the judges held that these activities could be regarded as legitimate business tactics.

Resale price maintenance was offensive to the newer types of retailers who found their enterprise frustrated by these devices for stereotyping the methods of sale. The large-scale multiples, the departmental stores, the co-operative stores and, in recent times, the supermarkets and the discount houses were strongly antagonistic. Some of them met the restrictions by developing their own brands and selling these as substitutes for the price-maintained goods of national manufacturers. The co-operative societies presented special problems. The dividends which they gave to customers on purchases were ignored by some associations. Others, however, regarded the dividends as a form of price-cutting, and they refused to allow the societies to give dividends on the goods supplied by their members. In general, opinion among economists was hostile to RPM, for they objected to a system of pricing which ignored differences in the costs of distribution. These restrictions on competition, they argued, hampered the transference of business from high-cost to low-cost retailers, led to the retention of excessive resources in retailing, and prevented the shopkeeper in a favourable location from passing on his economies to his customers. Admittedly RPM did not destroy competition, but it tended to substitute competition in service for competition in price. To those supporters of the system who claimed that in conditions of vigorous price competition adequate service could not be provided, the reply was given that the customer should be allowed the choice of buying that combination of goods and services which he preferred.

For many years after RPM had become a widely extended practice, Parliament saw no reason for disagreeing with the policy expressed in the decisions of the Courts. In 1931 a Board of Trade Committee on the Restraint of Trade surveyed the issues raised by RPM, but its report was inconclusive and no action was recommended. By the time the Lloyd Jacob Committee on Resale Prices reported in 1949, the climate of opinion had changed. Yet even that Committee, while condemning the collective enforcement of RPM, considered, with one dissentient, that arrangements for price maintenance between individual manufacturers and their distributors were generally innocuous from the standpoint of the public interest. There were plausible reasons for this distinction. It could be argued that individual manufacturers and retailers should be left free to trade as seemed to them best, and that as long as no one was compelled to adopt a uniform practice of trading, no harm was done. It was when traders were compelled by organized bodies to accept a certain method of doing business that the public interest was offended.

The signatory of the minority report recommended the abolition of both collectively enforced and individual resale price maintenance for reasons which we have already discussed. The Labour Government then in office was more favourably disposed to his recommendations than to those of the majority. In a White Paper issued in 1951 it proposed that all forms of RPM (except those related to the setting of maximum prices) should be made illegal, although there was to be provision for considering exceptional cases. The Government lost office before legislation could be introduced, and the next step forward was delayed until the passage of the Restrictive Trade Practices Act in 1956. The relevant clauses in that Act were much influenced (as will be seen presently) by the report of the Monopolies Commission on Collective Discrimination published in 1955. The Commission's terms of reference in that case had precluded it from surveying RPM as a whole and had obliged it to limit its attention to collective action. In its majority report the Commission recommended that collectively enforced RPM should be prohibited. This was consistent with its recommendations contained in several reports on particular industries. It is of some significance that up to this time the Commission had condemned individual resale price maintenance in only one case, pneumatic tyres. The reasons given for the exception were clear and explicit. In many of the industries surveyed, the Commission thought that, once the restrictive practices which it had condemned had been abandoned, there would be adequate competition among both manufacturers and retailers. In the pneumatic tyre industry, however, monopoly arose less from restrictive contracts among manufacturers than from the presence of price leadership which was not easily disturbed. So here the Commission hoped that increased competition among retailers for the goods of the several manufacturers would work back to the producers and loosen the grip of the price leader.

The argument that the removal of RPM might lead to more price competition among manufacturers was also used by the Monopolies Commission in a later report to justify their recommendation that the practice should be abolished. This was the report on the supply of electrical equipment for motor vehicles. The Commission also thought that the argument had some weight in the case of cigarettes, although there it concluded that RPM was not against the public interest. The reasons put forward to justify that conclusion as well as those advanced by the dissentient who took the contrary view throw light on the controversy. The defence of RPM in the sale of cigarettes rested on several arguments of which the following are the most important; first that the margins received by retailers were not in general excessive, secondly, that the abolition of RPM by leading to a transference of trade to cut-price shops might reduce the number of retail outlets to the inconvenience of customers, thirdly, that because of the very high incidence of tobacco duty, the extent of any possible price reduction would be small, and finally, that freedom in pricing would lead to 'loss-leader selling' which would bring about a still further concentration of production and so increase the extent of monopoly in the tobacco manufacturing industry.[1]

To the first argument the dissentient replied that the size of the *average* margins received by retailers was irrelevant; the significant fact was the divergence of costs among the various retailers in circumstances in which cost differences could not be reflected in retail prices. To the second argument he replied that he saw no reason why consumers should be prevented by the arbitrary decisions of the manufacturers from choosing how they should distribute their custom—as between buying their cigarettes at high-cost and high-price shops which might afford them some convenience of location and service, or at low-cost shops which were ready to pass on their economies to the purchasers. 'If resale price maintenance were abolished the number of retail outlets and the structure of this distributive trade would come to depend on the preference of consumers as expressed in the way they chose to spend their money, and not as at present on the manufacturers'

[1] Monopolies Commission, *Report on the Supply of Cigarettes and Tobacco and of Cigarette and Tobacco Machinery*, pp. 198–201.

dictate which frustrates their freedom of choice in one important respect.' If the number of outlets were reduced this would be because an insufficient number of customers was prepared to pay a price high enough to cover the costs of supplying them at certain high-cost points of sale—in other words, because of the effective competition of the low-priced shops. To the third contention that the amount of any possible price reduction would be very small the reply was given that the present habits of consumers had been moulded by the existing restrictive arrangements which offered no inducements for them to seek out low-cost distributors or to make purchases in quantity. If freedom of pricing were allowed, then shopkeepers in search of the advantage of a high turnover would be likely to reduce prices for purchases in quantity. To the final argument the dissentient replied that it could not be assumed that the present largest producer would be the chief beneficiary of freer pricing arrangements. Even if he were, it would be doubtful if restrictive practices should be kept in being and price competition excluded for the purpose of preserving a fringe of independent firms which, *ex hypothesi*, would be those which were unable to supply the market as effectively as the dominant producer or producers.[1]

Professor Yamey, in his criticism of the report, pointed out that the effects of 'loss-leader' selling as predicted by the Commission were the opposite of those which most defenders of RPM have regarded as the most probable. The Commission thought that the most popular brands would gain the chief benefits from 'loss-leader' selling to the detriment of other products, and that this would lead to further concentration of production in a few great firms. The usual argument is that the brand employed for 'loss-leader' selling ceases to be stocked by other than the price cutters with the result that its producer in the end suffers a loss of trade.[2]

Part II of the Restrictive Trade Practices Act introduced two

[1] Monopolies Commission, *Report on the Supply of Cigarettes and Tobacco and of Cigarette and Tobacco Machinery*, pp. 214–16.

[2] B. S. Yamey, *op. cit.*, pp. 49–50.

important changes in the law about RPM. First, collective action to prevent price cutting was prohibited, and secondly, the individual manufacturer was given the legal right to oblige retailers to adhere to his resale prices, even when the manufacturer had no direct contractual relations with them. This meant that the power of the manufacturers to enforce individual resale price maintenance was actually augmented. At first sight, these two provisions seem to be inconsistent with one another, but the explanation is not far to seek. The prohibition of collective action was in line with the recommendations of the Monopolies Commission and could be justified by the proposition that economic progress would be jeopardized if every firm was compelled to adopt the trading methods of the majority on its line if business. That argument clearly did not apply to individual RPM. The Government's decision not merely to tolerate that practice but actually to strengthen it was determined largely by an unwillingness to appear to discriminate against small firms. The abolition of the collective enforcement procedure made little difference to industries composed of a very few giant manufacturers who could police their own arrangements. But small firms were heavily dependent upon the collective enforcement machinery and could scarcely hope to preserve RPM without it. To increase the powers of legal enforcement was a means of redressing the balance between giant firms and others.

The Act exerted an important influence on methods of trading. Collective enforcement machinery was quickly dismantled and the associations that administered it were either dissolved or reconstructed with different rules. Yet, as already shown, in some industries efforts were made to preserve the substance of the old procedure by new devices, and many associations played an active part in assisting manufacturers in their individual actions against price cutters. In some industries a series of bilateral agreements between a manufacturer and his dealers was substituted for the former collective arrangements, and the trade associations took a prominent part in promoting this change. The Registrar, in an action brought in 1957 to deal with the registration of such agreements, pleaded that they constituted restrictive practices under the Act, but the Court found against him.

Where industries were in the hands of great firms with adequate enforcement procedures of their own, RPM continued much as before in the years after 1956. Elsewhere price-cutting became more common, and for some time this was encouraged by the failure of manufacturers to obtain injunctions against the offenders. Most of these failures, however, could be attributed to technicalities, and from 1962 onwards many successful actions were brought by manufacturers to restrain price-cutters. It has been estimated that between the passing of the Act of 1956 and that of the Resale Prices Act of 1964 more than 200 injunctions were obtained against price cutters.[1] In a far larger number of instances, suppliers had obtained voluntary undertakings from retailers to desist from price cutting without resort to a legal sanction.

As the change in the law coincided with important innovations in retailing which themselves had a close bearing on RPM, it is difficult to isolate the effects of the new law on competition. Thus, the spread of supermarkets during the later 1950s accompanied the breakdown of RPM in the grocery trade, and after 1960 discount houses, which relied for their business on cutting the prices of branded consumer durable goods, became of some importance. At one time it seemed possible that RPM would yield to these innovations in trading methods despite the legal reinforcement. Yet, although this remained true of the grocery trade, the law was successfully invoked on many occasions from 1958 onwards against price cutters in the chemists' trade, and after 1962 by the manufacturers of electrical goods and hardware to the discomfiture of the discount houses. It had, therefore, become clear by 1963–4 that, while some weakening in enforcement powers had occurred in several trades and more highly competitive conditions had appeared in a few of them, in the main the law had allowed manufacturers

[1] J. F. Pickering, 'The Enforcement of Resale Price Maintenance, 1956–64', in *Public Law*, autumn 1965, p. 236.

'to control price cutting without undue difficulty'.[1] Meanwhile, opinion in favour of encouraging increased competition among shopkeepers had gathered strength, for the spread of supermarkets revealed the economies to be obtained from newer types of retail organization. The outcome was the Resale Prices Act of 1964 which can be regarded as one of the most vigorous legal attacks on RPM to be found in any country.

Some features of the Act are analogous to certain clauses of the Restrictive Trade Practices Act. There is a general presumption that resale price maintenance is contrary to the public interest, but provision is made for suppliers to apply for exemptions from the general prohibition by reference to certain criteria set out in the Act. Exemption may be granted where the abolition of RPM would be detrimental to consumers for a number of reasons, namely that

1 the quality or variety of goods for sale would be substantially reduced;
2 the number of shops would be substantially reduced;
3 the prices of goods would be increased, in general and in the long run;
4 health would be endangered;
5 necessary pre-sales or post-sales services would be substantially reduced.

The above reasons for exemption, however, are subject to the proviso that the resulting detriment to consumers would outweigh the detriment to them of the continuance of RPM. This is equivalent to the 'tail-piece' in the Restrictive Trade Practices Act. It was also laid down that a supplier could not withhold supplies from a dealer on the ground that the latter had sold his goods at less than the recommended resale price. An exemption was permitted when the dealer had been found to use the supplies as 'loss-

[1] J. F. Pickering, 'The Enforcement of Resale Price Maintenance, 1956–1964' in *Public Law*, autumn, 1965, pp. 234–6.

leaders', although the definition of a 'loss-leader' is decidedly ambiguous.[1]

The Registrar was given important functions by the Resale Prices Act, comparable to those given to him by the 1956 Act. He was charged with the duty of compiling a register of suppliers who wished to claim exemption and of classifying them into appropriate groups. He was then required to bring cases selected from all the classes on his Register before the Court. Until the Court has made a decision about goods in a particular class, the suppliers of those goods are allowed to continue with RPM. When, however, its decision has been given in one representative case, that decision applies to all goods in the class.

Soon after the passage of the Act the price-cutting of maintained prices became widespread, even though shopkeepers who ignored the fixed prices risked the application of legal sanctions against them. Some of those who sought in this way to anticipate the decisions of the Court on applications for exemption from the ban were successfully proceeded against, but in general manufacturers now became less inclined than before 1964 to invoke the law against their defiant retail customers. Indeed, many of them, including some who have been strong supporters of RPM, decided to abandon the practice. Several important firms, however, registered claims for exemption, probably less because they themselves desired it, or saw much hope of succeeding in their claim, than because they believed that their loyal retail customers expected them to do so.

Among those who claimed exemption were leading manufacturers of chocolate and sugar confectionery who had from time to time, though not consistently, taken vigorous action against price cutting and had always affirmed their adherence in principle to RPM. Like cigarettes, confectionery is a product the sales of which are believed by manufacturers to depend on the existence of a large

[1] A 'loss-leader' transaction occurs when a resale of the goods is made by the dealer 'not for the purpose of making a profit on the sale of those goods, but for the purpose of attracting to the establishment at which the goods are sold customers likely to purchase other goods'. See Appendix C(iii).

number of retail outlets, and for this reason the producers felt that there was advantage in maintaining the uniform conventional margins. Their claim was the first on which the Court gave a decision. In July 1967 it held that the chocolate and sugar confectionery manufacturers had failed to make out a convincing case, and the practice had to be abandoned for all goods in that class. The Court's subsequent decisions so far have also been against the claims for exemption. It is still too early to affirm with certainty that RPM will not survive the legal attack. Yet the present indications are that the 'gateways' provided by the 1964 Act are even narrower than those of its predecessors.[1] If this proves to be so, then fresh opportunities for competition should now be available to the more vigorous or enterprising sections of the retail trade.

The policy of outlawing RPM may, therefore, make a substantial contribution to efficiency in British industry. The law itself, however, merely governs the environment within which firms operate. The abolition of collective enforcement by the 1956 Act had played a part in the breakdown of RPM in the grocery trade and a few others. But its chief function was that of clearing away the obstacles that had hitherto hampered innovators. At the time of that Act new forms of retailing were making their appearance, or were extending their scope, and the success of these ventures depended largely on the possibility of disregarding fixed prices or conventional margins. To some extent the new types of retailer could overcome the restrictions imposed by manufacturers by introducing their own brands, but they undoubtedly benefited by obtaining complete freedom in the pricing of all classes of branded goods. The producers for their part showed themselves susceptible to the pressure in favour of pricing freedom when this was exerted by major distributors.

If the new Act ultimately leads, as now seems probable, to the

[1] The Registrar decided not to oppose the claim of the Publishers Association for exemption. The Net Book Agreement, which provided for RPM, was registered under the 1956 Act and was upheld by the Court, as already stated. See p. 96 *supra*.

virtual abandonment of RPM throughout industry, it is reasonable to suppose that the more vigorous competition will bring lower average prices for the consumer. This result will be achieved by the transference of business from high-cost to low-cost distributors and by giving the enterprising firms freedom to introduce innovations in trading methods. A close observer of this aspect of monopoly estimated in 1960 that the price reductions that were to be expected from the abolition of RPM would amount to 5 per cent of current retail prices.[1]

[1] B. S. Yamey, op. cit., p. 15.

CHAPTER IX

Mergers and Monopolies of Scale

The Restrictive Trade Practices Act of 1956 affected both the structure and the operations of the Monopolies Commission. Until then the Commission's enquiries had been chiefly directed to cartels and restrictive agreements, and only a few monopolies of scale had been referred to it. The former now fell within the province of the Registrar and the Restrictive Practices Court, and the scope of the Commission's activities became more narrowly limited. The chief of its remaining functions was to enquire into the behaviour of dominant firms, the so-called monopolies of scale, and it was towards such investigations that it gave most of its attention after 1956, especially during the first few years. Yet, as a former secretary of the Commission has pointed out, whatever the practice, the law still allowed it a fairly wide diversity of function.[1] Apart from receiving references of monopolies of scale (which, of course, covered oligopoly as well as monopoly), the Commission was still empowered to deal with restrictive agreements about exports and agreements not registrable under the 1956 Act. It could also make (*a*) enquiries into compliance with its recommendations or into the due performance of undertakings given in pursuance of recommendations made in a previous enquiry, (*b*) general enquiries under Section 15 of the 1948 Act, similar in nature to that which led to the Report on Collective Discrimina-

[1] A. S. Gilbert, 'The System of Enforcement (2), the United Kingdom, (ii) The Monopolies Commission' in *Comparative Aspects of Anti-Trust Law in the United States, the United Kingdom and the European Economic Community*, pp. 58–60.

tion, and (*c*) enquiries into cases where the conditions of the 1948 Act applied because, without any agreement, suppliers responsible for one-third of a trade conducted their affairs so as to restrict competition. Price leadership and tacit understandings among oligopolists that lead to uniform pricing fall under the third heading.

Of the references dealt with by the Commission between 1956 and 1965, when the Monopolies and Mergers Act was passed, the following fall into the classification of monopolies of scale: (1) chemical fertilizers, (2) manufactured tobacco and cigarettes and cigarette-making machinery, (3) electrical equipment for motor cars, and (4) the processing of colour films. The enquiry into household detergents came under heading (*c*) above, and the enquiry into imported timber was concerned with the alleged non-compliance of the trade with undertakings given after a previous enquiry. The enquiry into the distribution of petrol had a rather unusual character. Normally the Commission had been required to investigate all the activities of a monopolist or oligopolist for the purpose of judging whether the 'things done' were contrary to the public interest. In this case, however, only certain activities of the petrol companies were brought under scrutiny, namely those concerned with the promotion of the 'solus site' selling of petrol. The wallpaper reference was in the same category. With the shrinkage of its responsibilities, the Commission's size was reduced and the panel system, which had permitted it to tackle several enquiries at the same time, was abolished.

Although after the 1956 Act the Commission ceased to count as the chief instrument of monopoly policy, its attention was now concentrated upon the most intractable problems in that field. Monopoly that arises from restrictive agreements among financially and legally independent firms can easily be identified. The economic consequences of the practices can be analysed and it is possible to judge with some confidence the results of their abolition. Even if the investigators begin their survey without any strong disposition in favour of market freedom, it is reasonable for them to require the industry to explain the reasons for any deliberate attempts that it may have made to destroy or curtail competition. Indeed, by the middle 'fifties the presumption that certain types of restrictive practices called for positive justification before they could be allowed to continue was fairly widely accepted by industry as well as by the general public, although admittedly this had not been so ten years earlier. It is true that when it came to finding remedies for restrictions judged harmful to the public interest, the mere abolition of the practices was not always a reliable method of creating vigorous competition, but at any rate the Commission could properly regard it as the first step. Thus, in dealing with restrictive practices, the Commissioners had certain principles to guide them and they could reasonably hope to be able to estimate the performance of an industry under alternative market conditions. When, however, they were confronted by monopolies of scale, the investigators were not armed by any set of generally accepted principles, and obvious alternatives to the existing structure were not as a rule easy to find.

This calls for further comment. The organization assumed by an industry is attributable in large measure to the nature of the market and the technique of production. If in a particular industry the economies of scale are considerable in relation to the size of the market, there may not be room for more than a very few firms, and those firms may have achieved their dominance by their superiority to rivals. The organization of such an industry cannot be disturbed without danger to its efficiency. Of course, great firms sometimes achieve their dominance not by superiority in production and marketing but by the use of restrictive devices which prevent the access of rivals to the markets. Where this is so, it may be assumed that the industry's performance will be improved by the abolition of those devices. A recommendation of this sort, however, does not always provide an easy solution of the problem. In some instances, a firm's dominance can be attributed to a combination of superior efficiency and restrictive practices. Or it may happen that, although a firm's dominant position can be traced to a deliberate policy of destroying its rivals by the use of restrictive measures, its present position can be justified by its performance or, at any rate, by the absence of any obvious alternative method of supply.

It was, therefore, very seldom that the Commission found itself able to prove decisively that a change in the organization of an industry would lead to superior performance. Clearly, if policy were to rest firmly on a presumption that more competition was always preferable to less competition and that 'performance' always yielded to 'market behaviour' as a criterion of judgment in this field, then the way forward would become less obscure. Yet even in the United States where these propositions have largely prevailed, the technical difficulties of handling monopolies of scale have proved very formidable and the American achievements in relation to them unimpressive. In the United Kingdom, in which those principles have not been accepted, the tasks of the Commission have been the more difficult. In effect, as we shall see presently, the Commission has been obliged to direct its attention chiefly to the practices of monopolists or oligopolists, and its recommendations have been concerned almost entirely with those practices rather than with organization as such. At any rate this was so until it became charged after 1965 with the duty of examining mergers.

A brief review of a few of the Commission's reports on monopolies will illustrate these general conclusions. Even before 1956 the Commission had encountered from time to time the problems which subsequently became its main concern. It had been called upon, for example, to examine the supply of industrial gases and matches, where single concerns were dominant, and it had reported on several industries where oligopolistic conditions and price leadership prevailed. However, in most of the industries in this last group the conditions were fortified by restrictive agreements and it was against these that the Commission aimed most of its criticisms. Industrial gases constituted the most clearly defined case of pure monopoly where the producer (British Oxygen) had not been content to rely on advantages of scale but had pursued a deliberate policy over many years of suppressing competition. The devices adopted for this purpose included control over the supply of plant and equipment, the taking over of other producers, the use of fighting companies to destroy rivals and the incorporation of exclusivity terms in contracts. The Commission condemned these practices and it found also that the producer had charged excessively high prices.[1] As remedies, it suggested that the Board of Trade should undertake periodical reviews of prices, costs and profits, while some members of the Commission proposed more drastic remedies, including nationalization. In none of these cases did the majority of the Commission go so far as to propose any change in the organization of the industry as by the disintegration of the dominant firm.

The first report of the Commission in its reconstituted form after 1956 dealt with chemical fertilizers.[2] This enquiry was from the beginning unsatisfactory since the Commission was precluded from examining the cartel arrangements which regulated the sale of ammonium sulphate. Such arrangements were now the province of the Restrictive Practices Court, but a fruitful enquiry into the industry obviously required that the conditions as a whole should be surveyed and not only certain aspects of them. In the chemical fertilizer industry two producers were responsible for the bulk of the main products; they were Imperial Chemical Industries and Fisons. Both of them sold their products at uniform delivered prices throughout England and Wales. Apart from one dissenting member who argued that this price policy, by deliberately breaking the link between costs and prices, led to a misuse of resources, the Commission acquiesced in this practice.[3] Its criticisms were confined to censuring Fisons who had incautiously admitted in evidence that

[1] *Report on the Supply of Certain Industrial and Medical Gases*, pp. 100–101.

[2] Strictly speaking, the first report was that on *Imported Timber*, but that report did not deal with a monopoly of scale.

[3] The charging of delivered prices is a characteristic of the Basing Point System, well known in the United States. According to this system the price quoted by steel makers, cement makers and other manufacturers in their sales to customers is composed of the factory price together with a charge for transport which is based, not on the actual cost of carriage, but on the cost from some designated centre, called a Basing Point.

their prices were fixed at a level that would provide the Company with resources necessary for carrying out its scheme of expansion into new fields. Fisons' prices and profits were, therefore, held to be excessive. For one type of fertilizer (potash) the Commission found that the firm responsible for the major part of the supply obtained the product from European concerns which themselves controlled prices by agreement. Fisons, the preponderant buyer of imported potash, owed its monopoly to its dominating position in the manufacture of compound fertilizers. The Commission thought that it was in a position to exert countervailing power in dealing with the European monopoly-suppliers and that this was in the public interest. But it also suggested that the Government and the chief fertilizer concerns should try to find other sources of potash so as to provide alternatives to the present suppliers.

Another obvious way of extending the area of competition is by the reduction of import duties. This is not a remedy which the Monopolies Commission has frequently put forward. Yet the advantages of overseas competition in the home market for the purpose of curbing domestic monopolists were stressed in the report on rubber footwear. In the case of colour films the Commission actually recommended that the import duty should be removed, but it is hardly necessary to say that this recommendation failed to win acceptance at the Board of Trade.

The report on cigarettes and cigarette machinery has several interesting features. In the first place, the Commission was critical of the performance of the chief producer mainly on the ground that it had failed to rationalize production and had kept in existence several uneconomic plants. This was a good example of a giant firm which, in the absence of competitive pressure, gave signs of having failed to seize opportunities for improving its efficiency. In the years immediately preceding the enquiry, however, the main producer had at last come under pressure from outside competition and had begun to respond.[1] Here there was a complication, for its

[1] Monopolies Commission, *Report on the Supply of Cigarettes and Tobacco, etc.*, pp. 188–9.

chief competitor was Gallahers of whose shares Imperial Tobacco held about 45 per cent. Although it appeared that Imperial had never attempted to use its holding to influence Gallaher's policy, the Commission thought that the financial relationship was undesirable and recommended that Imperial should dispose of its holding. This was the first time that the Commission had ever recommended such action. Partly because its implementation required an Act of Parliament, the Government rejected the proposal, but it obtained undertakings from Imperial which, in its opinion, served the same purpose. The Commission also recommended that Imperial's restrictions upon the freedom of its retail customers to display advertisements for competing brands should be abolished.[1] Thus, in this enquiry, the Commission reached a judgment about performance, and its remedies for the industry's deficiencies consisted in providing new stimuli to competition.

The report on equipment for motor vehicles is chiefly interesting because of its strictures on the practice of discriminating prices. In this industry the producers of most types of equipment sell a proportion of their output at low prices direct to the motor manufacturers for use as initial equipment, and the rest at much higher prices to the general public for replacements. The Commission reached the conclusion that whereas in the initial equipment market, the countervailing power of the buyers was a sufficient safeguard against the misuse of monopoly, in the replacement market there was no equivalent safeguard. It recommended that some competition might be infused into that section of the market by the abolition of resale price maintenance. The same recommendation was made in the report on wallpaper for similar reasons.[2]

It will be observed that, in the tobacco and the electrical equipment reports, the Commission concerned itself chiefly with the restrictive devices practised by the monopolists. In most of the

[1] For the Commission's views on resale maintenance in this trade, see pp. 108–9 *supra*.

[2] And also in the earlier report on pneumatic tyres; see p. 107 *supra*.

other references also it was the practices of the monopolist rather than the fact of dominance which excited criticism. These included exclusive dealing arrangements practised by suppliers of industrial gases and wallpaper, the withholding of supplies of components or machinery from competitors, as in the match industry, or the deliberate policy of absorbing rivals. In a few cases, as we have seen, the Commission recommended ways of curbing the power of monopolies by developing new sources of supply, as in the potash and match industries. The Commission gave attention to the record of monopolists in industrial research, but this was never regarded as more than contributory evidence in support of conclusions reached by other routes.

Even though the Monopolies Commission has been inclined to choose the safer line and to seek remedies in the abandonment of trade practices or the introduction of new competitors rather than in modifications of a monopoly-firm's structure, some of its decisions have been questioned, and not without justification. An instance of a widely-debated recommendation is to be found in the report on detergents. The manufacture of this product is largely controlled by two great suppliers who have competed, like oligopolists or duopolists in the conventional theoretical treatises, by raising selling costs rather than by price reduction. Among the selling costs, expenditure on advertisement holds a high place, and the Commission objected to it partly on the ground that it was wasteful and partly because it increased the difficulties of new firms that wished to enter the market. So, the Commission recommended that the expenditure on advertising these products should be restricted. This recommendation has been vigorously attacked. Advertisement, it is argued, is one of several marketing instruments, and it may be supposed that a firm's expenditure on the various instruments at its disposal is determined by its estimate of their relative effectiveness. If a firm is prevented by law from making use of its preferred instrument, then it will divert its marketing expenditure to others which, *ex hypothesi*, will be less effective in relation to cost. Distributing costs are, therefore, likely to be raised by restrictions on advertising as long as firms are left free in other respects to handle the marketing of their goods.

All the reports of the Commission contain detailed information about prices, costs and profits, but its judgments on the reasonableness or otherwise of the profits earned by monopolists have scarcely played a decisive part in determining its general conclusions. Profits have been calculated on capital employed. This has been based on the historical costs of the assets less depreciation and current liabilities. Firms have frequently challenged this method of arriving at profits and have claimed that replacement cost values were more satisfactory. The Commission's chief interest in calculating profits for particular industries has turned, however, on the possibility of making valid comparisons with industrial profits in general or with profits in certain industrial sectors. For this purpose historical cost is clearly the more appropriate method.

Even if the qualifications that surround all such comparisons are ignored, the difficulty of deciding whether the profits of a particular firm or industry have been reasonable remains formidable. Different industries require widely different rates of profit not only according to the risks to which they are exposed but also according to the extent to which they need resources for investment in research and development. The risk premium and the claims of research and development are matters of commercial judgment and are scarcely susceptible to any objective test that an outside body of investigators can readily apply. Nevertheless, the Commission did not always content itself with putting forward qualified conclusions when it found that a concern was earning a rate of profit well in excess of the average rate in circumstances in which it was largely immune from the risks of a competitive market. For instance, the profits of the British Match Corporation, British Oxygen and Champion Sparking Plugs were deemed to be unjustifiably high and, as already seen, this was also the judgment in the case of Fisons, although here there was strong supporting evidence. On the other hand, where a firm, though without rivals at home, earned very high profits chiefly by its success in competitive foreign markets (e.g. Molins, the manufacturer of cigarette machinery), the Commission found no cause for complaint. It also regarded with approval ICI's declared policy of aiming at higher profits in competitive markets than in those in which it enjoyed monopoly. Furthermore, the absence of high profits did not absolve the monopoly from criticism if the Commission thought that it had shown a lack of enterprise or that its organization was defective.

The principles that the Commission applied in attempting to reach decisions about profits are not open to question, but the determination of the reasonableness or otherwise of the actual rate of profit for a particular firm or industry is hardly within the capacity of any investigating body. Consequently, despite the prominence given to the cost and profit calculations in the reports, they usually played a modest part in influencing the Commission's findings in the monopoly cases as in the restrictive practices cases.

The governments of the 1950s did not retain a consistent interest in the monopoly problem, and they treated most of the recommendations of the Commission with scant respect. Indeed, much of the criticism directed against the Commission for the slowness with which it conducted its enquiries should properly have been turned on the Government which, after dallying with the reports, seldom gave the recommendations more than tepid support. During the later years of the Conservative Government's term of office, however, when the shortcomings of the economy were becoming increasingly obvious, public opinion began to favour a more vigorous policy. The action against resale price maintenance, as we have seen, was forceful. At the same time, the policy outlined in a White Paper on *Monopolies, Mergers and Restrictive Practices* issued in March 1964[1] showed that the Government was ready to fill other gaps left by earlier legislation. Apart from advocating that information agreements should be brought under the jurisdiction of the Restrictive Practices Court, the White Paper proposed an enlargement in the scope of the Monopolies Commission and an increase in the official powers to deal with its

[1] Cmnd. 2299.

recommendations. Powers were to be taken to break the financial links between the parties to a monopolistic enterprise when the public interest required it. The Monopolies Commission was also to be authorized to enquire into any proposed or completed merger which could lead to monopoly. Services as well as goods were to be brought within its purview.

The Conservative Government was not able to proceed with these proposals, but the Monopolies and Mergers Act passed in 1965, during the office of its successor, embodied an almost identical policy. In some ways the new Act went further than the original proposals. For instance, it gave the Board of Trade power not only to prohibit proposed mergers and to dissolve existing monopolies on the recommendation of the Commission, but also to delay the completion of any merger into which the Commission had been asked to enquire. Mergers subject to investigation were those that involved the take-over of assets worth more than 5 million pounds as well as those likely to lead to monopoly.[1] Thus size, as well as market dominance, was now to be called in question. The Act had special provisions for dealing with mergers among newspapers. Further, the Board of Trade was given the authority, on the Commission's recommendation, to require the publication of price lists and even to control prices. Services were brought within the Commission's ambit.[2] To deal with these increased responsibilities the Commission was enlarged and its power to work in panels was restored.

The action against mergers occurred at a time when British industry was being affected by a wave of combinations. It is doubtful if this could be attributed mainly to the efforts of firms to escape the provisions of the Restrictive Trade Practices Act, for many other forces were at work. But at least the new Act represented an

[1] Monopoly as defined in the 1948 Act; see p. 65 *supra*.

[2] Under this provision the Board of Trade in 1967 referred to the Commission the practice of certain of the professions. Apart from an earlier general reference (which was soon abandoned) on common prices, this was the first general reference since that which led to the report on collective discrimination.

attempt to deal with one of the most obvious methods by which firms intent upon avoiding competition could defeat the intentions of the earlier legislation. On the other hand, it has to be recognized that most mergers have little to do with efforts to establish monopoly. Many of them can be regarded simply as the adjustment of industry to meet new technical and marketing conditions by raising the scale of operation. Others involve movements towards vertical integration which may have no bearing on monopoly at all. In yet other cases, unsuccessful competitors may be taken over by their rivals as an alternative to bankruptcy. It is in a minority of cases that monopoly policy becomes concerned with mergers, but those cases are certainly numerous enough to require attention.

In several of its earlier reports, where the Monopolies Commission traced the development of great concerns, it expressed its disquiet at the process by which some of them had been built up. The very fact that the process of combination in an industry was difficult to reverse once it had passed into history suggested that it was in the public interest that there should be some investigation of mergers which might produce monopoly while these were in the formative stage. One of the chief difficulties in applying this principle lay in the fact that mergers likely to contribute to industrial efficiency might be held up or frustrated during the period of investigation. This difficulty has not been altogether removed by experience. It is true that the Commission has been able to present its judgments on mergers expeditiously, usually within a few months of receiving a reference from the Board of Trade, but so far it has been asked to handle very few cases.

Most of its enquiries—it had delivered seven reports up to January 1968—have led to recommendations in favour of the proposed mergers, and it has taken a contrary view in only two cases.[1] One of these concerned the proposed merger between United Drapery Stores and Montague Burton, the multiple tailors. The most important reasons for the rejection of this proposal were,

[1] These figures exclude reports on newspaper mergers which raise special considerations of policy.

first, that the merger was likely to reduce competition and to lead to higher prices and, second, that it was unlikely to make any significant contribution to improvements in efficiency.

Few would claim that the Commission is always capable of distinguishing beyond question between mergers which on balance will promote industrial efficiency and those which will have the reverse effect. But the judgments of a body of impartial and experienced investigators are indispensable to the sensible handling of this intricate problem. A real difficulty is that the work of the Commission in this field is clouded by an apparent ambiguity in official policy. On the one hand, the Government is trying to prevent combinations that restrict competition. On the other hand, it is intent upon creating in several British industries concerns of sufficient technological and financial strength to meet great foreign rivals on equal terms. For this purpose it has formed the Industrial Reorganization Corporation to encourage the consolidation of certain industries, and already this Corporation has had some successes. No one will deny that there is a valid distinction between 'good' and 'harmful' mergers, between those likely to open the way to increased efficiency and those likely to obstruct it. But not everyone believes that the Government, or outside bodies appointed by the Government, are always able to draw this distinction when confronted with actual industrial situations.

Up to January 1968 the Board of Trade itself had examined over two hundred proposals for mergers, while actual references to the Commission represented only about 3 per cent of that number. As the principles of selection have naturally not been made public, industrialists have contended that, in making plans for reorganization, they are left without any guidance about how their proposals might be received in official circles. This adds to uncertainties already present because of the activities of the Industrial Reorganization Corporation. Consequently, it is claimed, mergers that would have substantial advantages for the economy have been discouraged. The truth of these contentions is not easy to establish. No doubt some mergers have been discouraged, but whether these are mergers to which the Monopolies Commission would have given approval is much less certain. The existence of the machinery for scrutiny is most likely to have deterred the promotion of mergers of the kind to which it seemed, in the light of the Commission's reports, objection would be taken. However this may be, the Government has let it be known that, in order to remove these uncertainties, it is preparing a code for mergers. The provision of assistance for industrialists in their planning is not its only motive. It has been stimulated to take this action by pressure from the trade unions. Mergers that lead to a more efficient use of labour may cause local unemployment, at any rate temporarily, and a policy is required for dealing with that problem. The effect on employment is, of course, beyond the scope of this book. But a question which is highly relevant to the present study is whether the Government can draw up a set of principles which will really enable clear distinctions to be drawn between 'good' and 'bad' mergers.[1] If the code were to consist merely of a list of platitudes (corresponding to those descriptive of the public interest in the 1948 Act), industrialists will be left with their perplexities unresolved.

[1] The distinction is well brought out in the contrasting conclusions of two reports which appeared after this book had been finished. The Commission's report on Pilkington's monopoly of flat glass production praised the firm's efficiency and made no suggestion for modifying its domination of the trade. The report on man-made cellulosic fibres, however, contained several adverse criticisms of the monopolist, Courtaulds. First, the Commission held that the firm's policy of full-capacity working meant that, because of its monopoly, demand could not always be supplied at the peak and that this was a cost not fully offset by the firm's own economies in running full. (This criticism is the opposite of the usual charge against monopolists that their policies tend to create excessive capacity!) Secondly, the Commission found fault with Courtaulds' price policy, partly because its prices were high compared with those of some foreign producers, and partly because it discriminated in price when selling to its own subsidiaries. As remedies, the Commission proposed that tariffs should be reduced to increase foreign competition in cellulosic fibres and also that the firm should be restrained from its aggressive policy of acquiring other firms in the textile and clothing industries.

CHAPTER X

Monopoly Policy Abroad

I THE UNITED STATES

In the United States where modern industrialism met with few of the restraints that were elsewhere imposed by traditional society, policy towards monopoly and restrictive practices evolved earlier and achieved a higher degree of sophistication than in any other country. The home of the trust has not unnaturally been the breeding ground for anti-trust. Whereas in England and in some other countries the initial approach to the problem in modern times was tentative, the Americans almost from the beginning committed themselves to a definite principle which has informed most of their subsequent legal and administrative activities in regard to monopoly. Their policy in general, it may be said, was aimed at maintaining free competition and at frustrating efforts to restrict it. At the outset, it must be realized that this principle was never given universal application throughout the economy. As we shall see later, derogations from it have been permitted and widely recognized as justifiable for large classes of industries and transactions, e.g. agriculture, industries producing materials of strategic importance, such as oil-mining, public utilities, the retail trade, and trade union and professional activities. For private manufacturing industry and the wholesale trade, however, the principle has been applied without serious qualification. The competition of which we are now speaking refers to what may be called 'socially beneficial' competition as contrasted with 'unfair competition' designed to destroy or exclude competitors, although in practice this distinction has given rise to difficulties in law and administration.

If we look back to the origins of the policy, we observe that many strands of policy and opinion were joined in weaving the fabric of anti-trust. First, there was the common law, hostile as it once was in England to business conspiracy and to combinations in restraint of trade, but never a very effective means of curbing monopoly and restrictive practices. Secondly, we must note the American sentiment in favour of individualism and social egalitarianism. This sentiment was affronted by the predatory practices of the industrial magnates during the period after the Civil War, and especially by the discriminatory practices of the railway companies. Thirdly, there were the efforts of the 'publicists', including popular writers on economic questions, who roused the anger of the people against the magnates and brought to light the questionable activities of the ambitious trust-builders. Academic opinion on the trust question was at first rather indifferent. Many American economists were faithful to the *laissez-faire* prescription and deplored most forms of State intervention in economic life. Others believed that the underlying competitive forces in the economy were too strong to allow monopoly to survive. Even the few contemporary economists who were conscious of the strong trend towards monopolistic combinations in the later decades of the nineteenth century, and who realized the incompatibility of such structures with free competition, thought that potential competition would always be present in sufficient strength to prevent serious abuses. One of them, Ely, concluded that where the influence of potential competition was shown to be an inadequate safeguard, then public management was the answer. However, the academic economists were by no means favourably disposed towards monopoly itself, and later they rallied to the support of the anti-trust movement.

Hostility to monopolies had become sufficiently powerful in the later decades of the nineteenth century to persuade several States to take legislative action against them, but the first Federal Act was not passed until 1890. This was the famous Sherman Anti-trust Act. Since the Americans have preferred legal to administrative remedies for objectionable industrial practices we are obliged to discuss this legislation and successive measures at some length. The Sherman Act declared illegal (*a*) contracts, combinations or conspiracies in restraint of trade, and also (*b*) monopolizing, attempting to monopolize or conspiring to monopolize any part of the trade among the several States or with foreign countries. It was considered necessary to affirm under (*a*) the common law rule against restraint of trade because it was believed that no Federal common law existed on the subject. The immediate effects of this apparently strong legislative action were unimpressive, and several great consolidations leading to market domination occurred during the 1890s. The ineffectiveness can be explained by the absence of any official machinery for ensuring that the provisions of the law were carried out. At first, it was imagined that the Sherman Act would be 'self-enforcing', that aggrieved persons would bring charges before the Courts and that there was no need for continuous official regulation. The spread of monopoly during the 1890s disturbed public opinion, and the Government came to realize that the executive must take the initiative in enforcement. So, in 1903, a special division for the administration of the anti-trust law was set up in the Department of Justice. As a writer on the subject has stated: 'Anti-trust thus became institutionalized.'[1]

The Sherman Act still remains in force, although it has been subject to various amendments. For example, in 1937 the Miller-Tydings Act exempted from the condemnation of contracts in restraint of trade agreements which prescribed minimum prices for resale provided that the goods bore a trade mark or brand name and that they were in competition with others of the same class. This Federal Act extended to inter-State trade the 'fair trade' laws which had been passed in several individual States. Many of these laws provided (and still provide) that if a retailer entered into a 'fair trade' contract with a manufacturer, then all retailers in the State should observe the manufacturer's prices for those goods. In 1951 the Supreme Court decided that price maintenance con-

[1] H. B. Thorelli, *The Federal Anti-trust Policy*, p. 560.

tracts were binding in inter-State commerce only on those retailers that signed them, and that the so-called 'non-signer clause' in the laws of the individual States was invalid. The Federal Fair Trade Act of 1952 reversed this decision. This amendment did not, of course, authorize agreements between manufacturers about minimum resale prices or those between retailers. Further, no Federal law exists similar to the 'unfair practices' Acts which in several States prohibit selling below cost, that is to say, loss-leader selling. Nevertheless, the partial exemption of resale price maintenance from the legal attack provides for an important exemption from the general proscription of practices that restrict competition.[1]

Two other Federal Acts, both passed in 1914, completed the legal foundations of American monopoly policy. The Federal Trade Commission Act set up a Federal Trade Commission and provided for its methods of operation. As subsequently amended by the Wheeler-Lea Act of 1938, this legislation further declared unlawful the use of unfair methods of competition or unfair or deceptive practices in commerce, although RPM agreements were again exempt. The Commission was given extensive duties. Like the British Monopolies Commission, it concerns itself with collecting information about business operations, and, unlike its British counterpart, it may itself initiate these enquiries. It also investigates violations of the Sherman Act. On application by the Attorney General it may recommend modifications in business practices to bring them into conformity with the law; and it scrutinizes the results of anti-trust decisions. Whereas the Sherman Act, which created criminal offences, may be enforced by actions instituted by

[1] However, the debate is not over. In seven or eight of the States with Fair Trade Acts the enforcement of RPM against 'non-signers' no longer enjoys statutory protection. Moreover, Congress has been recommended by the Attorney General's National Committee to Study Anti-trust Laws (*Report*, March 1955) to repeal the Acts permissive of resale price maintenance, including the Miller-Tydings and the Federal Fair Trade Acts. See A. D. Neale, *The Anti-trust Laws of the United States of America*, pp. 353–4.

the Department of Justice, the Federal Trade Commission must confine itself to civil proceedings. It normally enforces its decisions by issuing 'cease and desist' orders on offenders. However, the distinction between proceedings under the two Acts is apparently not as great as might be supposed. Thus, the Department of Justice under the Sherman Act may institute equity proceedings to restrain violations of the law, and it may issue regulations about the future conduct of the offending business, while the Federal Trade Commission is competent to deal with certain cases (e.g. those concerned with 'unfair competition') which are virtually identical with cases covered by the Sherman Act.

The second of the Acts passed in 1914, the Clayton Act, declared illegal four specified practices when their effect might be substantially to lessen competition or to tend to create a monopoly. These were (1) price discrimination, (2) exclusive dealing arrangements and tying contracts, (3) acquisition of shares in another company, and (4) interlocking directorates. An amendment, the Robinson-Patman Act of 1936, strengthened the law against price discrimination by extending the prohibition to discrimination in discounts, and it forbade the sale of goods at unreasonably low prices for the purpose of eliminating competitors. The Anti-Merger Act of 1950 extended the prohibition of share acquisitions in other companies to cover the purchase of physical assets, again in cases where the effect might be substantially to lessen competition or to create a monopoly. In addition, various sanctions can be invoked against foreign firms which, in their trade with the United States, or with importers, attempt to limit competitive freedom. The Wilson Tariff Act of 1894 declared illegal any combinations or conspiracies in restraint of trade among importers. The Anti-Dumping Regulations forbade the import and sale of articles at prices substantially less than the market or wholesale price with the intent of injuring an American industry or of monopolizing any part of the trade. Additional duties can be levied on articles imported under exclusive dealing arrangements.

It is evident that the American anti-trust law rests squarely on the principle that free competition is good and that movements towards monopoly are to be resisted. This principle was not, of course, derived from economic reasoning or from a close examination of the economic effects of competition and monopoly. It represented rather a political judgment about the value of a particular form of economic organization. Indeed, the policy as a whole cannot be understood without reference to the attitude of Americans towards their society in all its aspects and towards the relationships of individuals within that society. It must be emphasized again, however, that this principle has been permitted a restricted application. The price support schemes for agriculture and the legal defence accorded to RPM accord ill with the deference paid by the law to competition in manufacturing and wholesale trade. An explanation of the paradox is not hard to find. The policies just mentioned as exceptional rest primarily on a desire to support the 'little man', especially the farmer and the small retailer. Thus, American opinion is not concerned simply with sustaining competition because it is believed to provide a necessary stimulus to efficiency and progress. It also insists that efforts shall be made to preserve a large number of independent business units, because these are believed to be socially and politically desirable. The free market system is by no means always compatible with this aim, for unrestrained competition may sometimes lead to the supremacy of the most successful competitor. Where such a conflict arises, the principle underlying monopoly policy loses something of its grand simplicity. In some spheres, where the economies of scale seem to be overwhelming, the principle is adhered to. But in agriculture and retail trade the vote is cast in favour of restraining competition in the interests of the survival of numerous small units. This decision again brings out the fact that the American anti-monopoly policy rests upon a political rather than an economic judgment.

Certain other exceptions to the principle can be justified, or at any rate explained, by reference to the national as distinct from the general interest or to special economic circumstances. For instance, the Webb-Pomerene Act of 1918 exempted associations engaged solely in the export trade from the provisions of the Sherman Act. This exemption was designed to enable exporters to exert monopolistic powers when confronting foreign sellers, and, by making possible the avoidance of competition among firms in the same trade, to assist in improving the American terms of trade. During the Great Depression of the 1930s, President Roosevelt's National Recovery programme led for a time to a virtual suspension of anti-trust policy and to deliberate efforts on the part of the Government to increase the price-fixing powers of associated producers. This was an example of the anti-depression cartels that are found in a number of countries where the law is otherwise hostile to restrictive practices.

Despite these important exclusions, within the greater part of industry and trade the prohibitions on restrictive practices are comprehensive and drastic. Collusion over prices, sales and markets among independent firms is illegal. Patent rights cannot be used for the purpose of extending the officially conferred monopoly by agreement with the licensee. Nor is evidence of overt collusion necessarily required by the Courts, which apply a doctrine of 'implied conspiracy'. This means that the collusion may be inferred from market behaviour, as when several sellers are found to be charging identical prices ('conscious parallelism') or when a firm practises systematic price discrimination. The doctrine raises awkward problems for oligopolies. These are naturally disposed towards collusion over prices so as to avoid disastrous price wars, and they can often achieve their aims without explicit agreements with one another. A tacit understanding, however, may be inferred from market behaviour and may lay the firms open to attack.

Price discrimination, as we have seen, was expressly excluded by the Clayton Act from legitimate pricing methods whenever the effect was substantially to lessen competition. In practice this rule has given rise to many complications. The Courts have met with difficulties in applying the law and have been obliged to permit exceptions. For instance, where the lower price charged by a firm that is practising price discrimination has been made in order to meet competition, the Court has acquiesced. In doing so it has clearly opened a wide path to derogations from the rule. The rule leads to more serious complications when it encounters the modern pricing policies of a great concern. Such a concern is unlikely to meet competition, or to mount an attack on a rival, by introducing sweeping changes in prices applicable to all customers for its whole range of standard products. If it were to do this in an oligopolistic industry, it might provoke a price war. In any event the effect on the volume of demand and on profits would be incalculable. So it usually prefers to sharpen its competition by introducing new varieties of its product and to conceal price changes within the altered structure of its output. In some cases it may limit these changes to a particular sector of the market. If this policy is successful, then the experiment may be the precursor of widespread price adjustments.

One might say that a great firm tends to start a period of intenser competition by resorting to various kinds of discriminating devices and in this way avoids committing its whole position. If the law were to prevent price discrimination practised in these circumstances, competition might even be discouraged and prices made more rigid. In other words, some types of price discrimination may be properly regarded as a form of price competition. On the other hand, there can be little doubt that price discrimination is in other circumstances to be regarded as a monopolistic device designed to destroy competition. An American commentator has stated that public policy in this sphere walks a tight-rope; it must try to distinguish between the price discrimination that assists competition and that which undermines it.[1] The trouble is that policy is interpreted by judges who must proceed according to legal rules. The distinction with which we are here concerned, however, is an economic distinction which can be identified only after detailed

[1] E. H. Chamberlin (Ed.), *Monopoly and Competition and Their Regulation*, p. 133.

investigation of the actual effects of the price discrimination in each case.

The prohibition of restrictive practices and of monopolistic behaviour by individual firms is so strictly enforced that groups of manufacturers who wish to avoid competition are given every inducement to form close combinations. Or, a firm that wishes to put an end to another's rivalry has a strong incentive to absorb its rival, although it must, of course, refrain from unfair means of competition in the process of achieving this result. Yet even if a firm reaches a position of market dominance solely by reason of its superior efficiency, it is by no means immune from legal attack. Here one arrives at one of the most difficult problems in the field of monopoly policy, and it cannot be said that the Americans, for all their pertinacity and long experience, have been conspicuously successful in solving it.

In the first place, it is significant that the application of the law to close combines has varied from time to time. In the early years of this century vigorous action was taken against a number of giant trusts which were in fact broken up in consequence of Court rulings. During the boom of the 1920s the combines were viewed with complacency. Size or market dominance at that time was not in itself a reason for disapproval. In those years anti-trust policy directed its attention mainly to the devices used for establishing a monopoly and to the way in which power once achieved was exercised. The Rule of Reason, as it was termed, was then concerned with whether a monopolistic organization was beneficial or not in its operations, and whether it had used its power to injure rivals. The accepted doctrine seemed to be epitomized in the words of a judgment in the case of the United States Steel Corporation in 1920: 'The law does not make the mere size of the Corporation an offence; or the existence of unexerted power an offence when unaccompanied by unlawful conduct.' The conduct which the Court had in mind referred mainly to the treatment of rivals. In the case in question the firm was not held to have used its power badly and so it escaped condemnation.

After the Second World War there was a marked change of emphasis. A new era in anti-trust policy was signalized by the judgment in the Alcoa case of 1945 when it was declared that no distinction existed between 'good' and 'bad' monopolies, and that 'power and its exercise must necessarily coalesce'. Yet, whereas in the early years of the century when a similar doctrine prevailed the Court found a remedy in the breaking up of trusts, during the last twenty years the Court has been reluctant to disturb the corporate *status quo* and there have been few instances of divestiture. The reason is that it is now realized that to take action after a monopoly has been created is too late. Efforts must be directed towards preventing its formation. Consequently, the most vigorous action has been directed against mergers intended to lessen competition and against restrictive practices by monopolists (as the British would say, against the 'things done' for the purpose of creating or maintaining the monopoly). The tendency is to deal with these blemishes by the issue of 'cease and desist' orders. It should be added that the Court has certainly tended in recent years to take a stricter view than formerly of what does in fact substantially lessen competition.

Another reason why there is now less inclination than in the past to break up established monopolies is that today oligopoly rather than monopoly has become the chief issue. Further, great size in recent decades has been achieved by a process of internal growth at least as much as by mergers. Consequently, the old remedy of dissolution is less appropriate, since where monopoly has been achieved by internal growth the presumption is that it has been attained by superior efficiency. It still remains true, however, that, unlike the British in their dealings with monopoly and restrictive practices, the administrators of the American anti-trust policy have not been deeply concerned with a firm's or an industry's *performance*. They regard as axiomatic the proposition that more competition is to be preferred to less competition, and they, therefore, concentrate their attention on structures or practices that are monopolistic in tendency. In reaching judgments the test applied by the Court is the effect of the 'things done' or the structure under investigation on competition rather than on the industry's contribution to economic welfare or to its performance.[1] Indeed, according to one writer, what the application of the Rule of Reason now involves is that the Court has to decide whether the market is 'workably competitive'. If the market lacks this quality, the Court must consider what changes in structure or market behaviour are required in order to introduce or restore it.

While American anti-trust policy is obsessed with changes in the degree of competition, it is troubled by questions of size only when the magnitude of an organization tends to create a monopoly in any line of business. A multi-product firm may be huge without being a monopolist in any product or market. When it comes to a consideration of a firm's dominance, it is necessary to define precisely what it is that is said to be monopolized. In other words, attention must be given to the effectiveness of substitutes, to cross elasticities of demand. Du Pont monopolized the production of cellophane, but when the case was brought before the Court its lawyers argued that the relevant commodity was 'wrapping material' in the production of which many independent firms were engaged. This contention was accepted by the Court.

One may conclude that American policy has been successful, without question, in its application to cartels and restrictive practices, but despite a long experience the complicated issues raised by

[1] Some commentators on the Alcoa case have declared that, although the Court based its adverse decision mainly on the extent of the Company's domination of the market, it was also influenced by the way its power had been used, that is to say, the Court took account of the Company's aggressive behaviour. These are nice questions for lawyers, but to the layman it does not seem easy to distinguish between aggressive behaviour (when unaccompanied by restrictive practices) and ordinary successful competition. Both leave diminished opportunities for other firms or newcomers. In any case, this question of acceptable conduct (in the above sense) is hardly identical with that of the firm's efficiency in production and marketing which is the commonly understood meaning of 'effective business performance'. Cf. E. S. Mason, *Economic Concentration and the Monopoly Problem*, pp. 358–61.

the presence of great dominating firms have not been solved. Some commentators have observed that the Courts, when confronted with giant concerns, have been increasingly inclined to content themselves with lecturing their administrators on acceptable behaviour, a form of anti-monopoly policy commonly known as 'jaw-bone regulation'. The British, with a long experience of official exhortation, are likely to share the scepticism of many Americans about this method of controlling monopoly.

2 THE EUROPEAN ECONOMIC COMMUNITY

Until recently the governments of Continental Europe have regarded monopoly and restrictive practices without marked hostility. Some of them have adopted a permissive attitude and have intervened only for the purpose of dealing with obvious abuses. Others have actually encouraged cartels and dominating industrial organizations as instruments of economic growth or efficient administration. It appears that the general disposition of the various countries towards freedom in the political sphere has exerted a comparatively slight effect on the extent to which restrictive practices or combines have prevailed. Thus, the French Penal Code of 1810 (Article 419) had, in effect, condemned all agreements in restraint of trade; but this did not prevent their proliferation during the next hundred years, for the Courts drew a distinction between 'good' and 'bad' *ententes* (cartels) with the result that only the few which were proved to have raised prices excessively were condemned. An amendment of the Penal Code in 1926 declared illegal certain specified devices for manipulating markets, but in practice the law continued to treat most restrictive agreements with toleration. Soon after the Second World War the monopoly problem attracted attention in France as in other countries. Laws were passed to prohibit the fixing of minimum prices for goods and services (except for branded goods) and to supervise the practices of cartels. Later, in 1958, resale price maintenance was declared illegal. So it is evident that in the years before the formation of the

European Economic Community the French law was becoming more hostile to monopolistic practices, although it is doubtful if all these efforts of the authorities to maintain or restore competition were effective. For instance, the main strength of the attack on *prix imposés* (RPM) came not from the law but, as in Great Britain, chiefly from the new types of distributors who followed a deliberate policy of price cutting.

In the German legal system there was no equivalent to the English common law doctrine of the unenforcibility of contracts in restraint of trade or to Article 419 of the French Penal Code. The Courts almost invariably conceded the validity of cartel agreements and enforced manufacturers' conditions of sale against price-cutting retailers, even if there were no contract between them. In the period in which Germany was establishing herself as a leading industrial nation, the State on the whole looked with favour on the development of great concerns, or strong associations of industrialists, on the ground that these might effectively confront foreign competitors. During the great inflation after the First World War there was a change of attitude. Cartels became unpopular and in 1923 a Cartel Decree was issued which, while accepting these associations as necessary features of industrial life, purported to prevent any abuse of monopoly power. The Decree covered cartels, exclusive agencies and resale price maintenance. It also provided for the establishment of a Cartel Court the chief function of which was to assess the economic consequences of particular restrictive practices. Where the Court found that a cartel had abused its powers, then it could declare the agreement null and void.

After the Second World War the economic policy of Germany was for a time determined by the Allies, and ordinances were issued designed to break up many of the great concerns and to maintain competitive conditions throughout German industry. The deconcentration policy, however, was far from achieving its ambitious aims. When Germany again resumed control over her economic affairs, she adopted towards cartels and dominating concerns a generally permissive policy which, nevertheless, provided for legal action to be taken against them in cases of the abuse of monopoly power. It was consistent with this attitude that the Law on the Restriction of Competition should have permitted the resale price maintenance of branded goods. Yet one cannot judge the facts of an economic situation simply by reference to legal enactments and administrative machinery. On the face of it, the French authorities in the post-war period might seem to have taken a more hostile attitude towards restrictions on competition than the Germans, but it would be rash indeed to conclude that in that period France possessed the more vigorously competitive economy. Other factors besides the law influenced the market and the behaviour of firms.

The legal attitude to monopoly in other European countries must be briefly summarized. In Belgium the legislation has been favourable to the formation of cartels and combines. Although in principle some supervision was exerted over their operations with the object of preventing abuses, in practice most of their activities were tolerated. In Holland an Act of 1935 gave the Government power both to enforce on all members of a trade certain agreements concluded by a majority and also to dissolve agreements considered contrary to the public interest. The provisions of this Act were extended during and immediately after the Second World War, but it is doubtful if they exerted much effect on industrial behaviour. In Italy, during the period of Fascist rule between the wars, cartels were regarded as organs of the Corporative State and consequently were encouraged and even made obligatory. After the war the Fascist legislation was repealed and some provision was made for the supervision of cartels. Switzerland had no legislation to deal specifically with restrictive agreements or with monopolies. The opinion has prevailed that, despite the evident disadvantages of cartels, these were to be preferred to the State intervention in economic life which an anti-monopoly policy would bring with it. The legal toleration of restrictive practices has encouraged numerous international cartels to set up their headquarters in certain Swiss Cantons (e.g. Glarus) and in Liechtenstein.

The formation of the European Economic Community profoundly affected policy towards monopoly and restrictive practices throughout all the member countries. The economic benefits of a Common Market were to be secured in part by a reduction of trade barriers among the Six so that Europe could enjoy the advantages of large-scale and specialized production denied to producers for limited national markets. The area of competition was to be enlarged and economic policies within the group harmonized. But, as we have seen, cartels flourished in all the member countries; some of them were national in scope while others were composed of firms in several countries. Their operations were clearly incompatible with the existence of a free European market. As was stated in a report of the EEC Commission in July 1962: 'It would be useless to abolish trade barriers between the member States if they and private industry were left free, through legislation in the fiscal or economic fields, through subsidies or understandings which restrict competition, to frustrate the movement towards the widening of the market.' The need for a policy on competition arose, therefore, from the objectives of the Common Market itself. It was accepted, in fact, by the signatories of the Treaty of Rome that competition should play an important role 'as an instrument of guidance for the co-ordination of the Community's economic progress'. A common policy towards monopoly and competition lay at the foundation of the new venture.

The acceptance of this principle, however, left many practical problems unsolved. For instance, at the outset the disparities among the various member States in their legislation on monopoly and competition, and the virtual lack of any such legislation at all in two of them (Italy and Luxembourg) was a serious obstacle to the evolution of policy. Only three of the countries (France, Germany and Holland) possessed an administration for dealing with these matters, and only in Germany, with its Federal Cartel Office, was the administration well developed. National forms of administration, therefore, as well as *supra*-national machinery, had to be created before the policies could take effect.

In one sector of the industrial field, however, an advance had already been made. The first step towards the European Common Market had been taken with the signing of the Paris Treaty in 1952 which established the European Coal and Steel Community. A discussion of this organization lies beyond the scope of this book, but its purpose must be mentioned inasmuch as one of its aims was the abolition of restrictive practices among the coal and steel producers of the six member countries and the creation of conditions which would 'assure the most rational distribution of production at the highest possible level of productivity'. The contraction of the European coal industry and the depressed conditions encountered in the middle 'sixties by the steel industry forced the High Authority of ECSC to introduce measures of compromise and to permit practices hardly compatible with the original principles. But the Authority has tried to minimize the extent of this retreat from competition and to retain close control over any restrictive practices which it has felt bound to permit. The founders of the European Economic Community in the late 'fifties had, therefore, some experience to guide them in framing policies towards monopoly.

In accordance with the general principle of encouraging free competition within the boundaries of EEC the practices prohibited by the Treaty of Rome and subsequent Regulations, included the fixing of common prices, market sharing, restrictions on production or technical development and discriminatory supply conditions, where these were likely to affect trade between the member States. The Treaty does not condemn monopolies as such, but only the abuse of a dominant market position, again in cases where the monopolist's operations affect two or more of the member countries. It should be emphasized that the rules do not cover restrictive practices that apply to the internal trade of a particular country, and for this reason policy in regard to RPM continues to differ among the several members. However, to the extent that the single market is substituted for the national market, it is to be presumed that the distinction between what is of internal concern and what is of common interest will ultimately disappear.

Certain 'Rules of Competition' were set out in Articles 85 and 86 of the Treaty of Rome, and later in Regulations issued by the Council and the Commission of EEC. Article 85 prohibits agreements, arrangements and practices which prevent, restrict or disturb competition within the Common Market and affect trade between the member States, while Article 86 prohibits the pursuit of unfair or improper practices by a dominant firm if these impair trade among the member States. Article 85 provides a 'gateway' to permit the continuance of arrangements which are proved to promote technical or economic progress, but this toleration is qualified by the provision that consumers must be allowed a reasonable share of the benefits of such progress and that the arrangements must not be destructive of competition over a substantial part of the market for the goods. Certain goods and services are excluded, though not unconditionally, from these rules, namely those with the character of a fiscal monopoly, those for which the European Coal and Steel Community and the European Atomic Energy Community are responsible, and agricultural products.

The authorities responsible for the enforcement of the rules are the Commission of EEC whose decisions are subject to verification by the Court of Justice, and also the judicial and administrative authorities of the member States. It has been necessary to ensure close co-operation between the Commission and national authorities, especially during the early period of the Common Market's existence, in order to bring the various national policies into harmony and to avoid inconsistent rulings. Originally it was intended to provide for the compulsory registration of all cartels and restrictive agreements, but this proposal was modified in favour of an arrangement by which those who wished to maintain prohibited practices were required to notify the Commission. If the Commission were satisfied that these practices were beneficial according to the criteria laid down in Article 85, then it could grant clearances to the firms or associations concerned. The Commission can impose heavy penalties for infringements of the rules and it has wide powers of inspection.

Since December 1961 when the Treaty came into effect, the Commission and the Court of Justice have been actively engaged in applying the general rules, and on the basis of their decision a body of case law is being built up. Much of the Commission's attention has been directed to the problem of exclusive dealerships, by which a manufacturer restricts the sale of his goods in a country other than his own to a single firm. It has finally been decided that the prohibition on such dealerships should apply to arrangements by which manufacturers of competing products give each other exclusive rights of sale in their respective countries. Consequently, it gave a block exemption from the prohibition to exclusive dealing arrangements which did not restrict competition in this way, and it excused those who were parties to them from registering their arrangements. This practice of granting block exemptions has been applied to other restrictions also. Some 20,000 agreements have been notified, and the Commission's policy has been to classify these into groups and to exempt from control those considered inoffensive to competition. This procedure no doubt reduces the problem of administration to manageable proportions. It bears some resemblance to that provided for in the British Resale Prices Act of 1964.

In spite of all the efforts of the last decade, there are still discrepancies among the policies of individual governments, and the Commission has not found it easy to achieve conformity. Not unnaturally the Commission's attitude towards restrictions on competition is more downright and legalistic than that of most of the member countries towards the cartels and monopolies that operate only within their national boundaries. Britain's anti-monopoly policy at present is certainly more hostile to restrictive practices than that of any of the individual members of EEC (although perhaps not, in principle, more so than that of the Commission), but the problem of adjusting British methods of treatment to those of Europe does not now appear to require an early solution. While it is probable that the most useful task of the Commission lies in preventing firms from thwarting by private arrangements the results of trade liberalization among members of the Common Market, this is not the limit of its responsibilities. Thus, an important obstacle to keener competition within the community is found in the lack of standardized specifications for many classes of finished product or their components. Electrical apparatus provides a good example. If the authorities could standardize specifications for that type of apparatus, competition would become more perfect throughout the community.

Lately, the Commission has been confronted with some difficult problems of economic judgment. The EEC countries face the same dilemma as Great Britain in dealing with great aggregations of economic power. While the Common Market authorities are intent upon stimulating competition and avoiding the dangers attendant upon market dominance, they are at the same time anxious that their industrial firms shall be large enough to have full access to the economies of scale. This is especially important if European industries are to compete effectively with great producers whose interests are mainly outside the EEC, although they may have a foothold within it. For instance, in the man-made fibres industry the competition which now counts is that among the few giant chemical companies with international interests. It is for this reason that various derogations from the rules against monopoly are now being proposed. In such circumstances it is as well that a wide discretion should be allowed to the authorities, for a decision in every case is likely to depend on a nice balance of advantages and disadvantages.

CHAPTER XI

Conclusions

It would be otiose to try to summarize in a concluding chapter the narrative and arguments of the book, but it may be useful to emphasize the outstanding features of the policy which has been our concern. First, let us discuss the nature and necessity of this policy in modern industrial societies, with particular reference to the United Kingdom; next, let us consider the relative importance of the different instruments that have been employed in the execution of the British policy; and finally, within the acknowledged limits of reasonable expectations, let us reflect on some of the suggestions put forward for making the policy more effective.

Sir Henry Clay, an economist sympathetic with the business point of view, voiced his disapproval of the British Government's post-war monopoly policy, then in its early stages, by insisting that it discriminated strongly against private manufacturing industry and trade. The British industrialist or merchant, he said, in effect, was obliged to buy most of his fuel and transport services from public monopolies, his labour in a market dominated by trade unions and distorted by restrictive practices, and many other services from the highly organized professions which laid down conditions of supply for their members. Some of the raw materials he needed were controlled by monopolistic marketing bodies, official or semi-official. And when he had to deal, as a harsh fate was impelling him increasingly to deal, with bureaucrats and politicians, he found himself confronted by persons secure from the vulgar pressures of the market place. Why should the manufacturer and merchant be expected to accept highly competitive conditions for their own operations in a world otherwise given over to monopoly? Why should *their* restrictive practices alone be singled out for condemnation? These questions, which might be posed in other countries, as well as in the United Kingdom, cannot be lightly brushed aside, but there is an answer to them.

While it may be agreed that the principle of competition should not be limited in its application to manufacturing industry and trade, it does not follow that this principle has everywhere the same wide application, or that identical administrative or judicial arrangements for controlling monopoly and restrictive practices are equally suitable for all classes of transactions. Trade unions have long been defended on the ground that the individual worker is at a disadvantage in bargaining with his employer and that only by combination with his fellows can he secure parity of strength. The same argument has been used to justify restrictive practices among producers of agricultural raw materials and foodstuffs. These are for the most part small people who, as individuals, cannot meet the dealers on equal terms. By combining together for the sale of their products, they may hope to establish 'countervailing power' against the massive strength of the large purchasers. This defence does not, of course, justify situations in which the power so created is abused, or in which the forms of organization have become obsolete or mischievous. In that event it may be necessary to impose public control over these bodies, but even so it does not follow that the machinery of regulation will be identical with that used for handling similar situations in manufacturing industry or trade. Light may be thrown on some part of this problem by the forthcoming Report of the Royal Commission on the Trade Unions. As to the professions, the organs that regulate the conditions in which their services are supplied are chiefly occupied in maintaining certain standards of integrity and performance, and their restrictive arrangements have been justified for that reason. However, the reference in 1967 of the practices of some of the professions to the Monopolies Commission shows that they are no longer immune from inquiry.

Public monopolies for their part are often (popularly) held to inhabit a different realm from that of private monopolies, for they are supposed to be primarily concerned with satisfying the needs of the public and not with profit-seeking. Any remedy for their deficiencies can be supplied, so it is argued, by the Government or Parliament. The British consumers of the products of the nationalized industries have now had twenty years in which to judge the validity of this apologia and, in particular, the effectiveness of Parliamentary control over the public sector. Fortunately, we need not debate the question, since, during the last two decades, technical and commercial changes have largely undermined the market power of many of the State monopolies. The National Coal Board, which originally supplied the bulk of the fuel used in Great Britain, now has to compete for its dwindling share of the fuel and power market with several other industries. These include, among the suppliers of primary fuels, the privately owned oil and natural gas industries and the publicly owned atomic power industry. The nationalized electricity and gas industries compete with each other as well as with the coal and oil industries. The nationalized railway industry has retreated before the competition of road and air transport, and the nationalized air services are challenged by private air companies, despite the limitation officially imposed on the latter's sphere of operations. Competition is thus by no means excluded from the public sector of the economy and, unless it is deliberately frustrated, it can be expected to make a contribution to satisfactory performance.

The private manufacturer and merchant are, therefore, not quite so exceptional in this respect as is sometimes supposed, and the contrast between the treatment accorded to their activities and to other categories of transactions may not be as great as Sir Henry Clay once thought. In any case the arguments in favour of a more competitive system in industry and trade are not refuted by stressing the difficulty of its universal extension or of securing uniformity in methods of enforcing policy. Even the most ardent advocates of the competitive principle are willing to exclude certain fields from its application; at the same time it may be necessary to devise different methods of regulation adapted to the special circumstances of particular types of monopoly.

The reasons why it has been found expedient in this and other countries to introduce control over various forms of monopoly and restrictive practices have been examined in earlier chapters, but something more must be said. First of all, it must be emphasized that the reasons are not derived from economics alone. Policy towards monopoly depends on the values accepted by a society, and in the end it can be defended only by reference to those values. A policy antagonistic to monopoly cannot rest on the proposition that competition is 'natural', for the unconstrained evolution of economic arrangements leads to monopolistic as well as to competitive structures. Nor can it be based on the desirability of perfect competition, for this is a conceptual device of economic analysis and does not represent a social judgment. The rules of business behaviour to be prescribed are purely empirical. If we wish to enjoy rapid economic progress, to avoid exploitation in market transactions, and to prevent a high concentration of economic power, we must ask: what system is most successful in producing these results? As we have seen, the test of experience, though it leaves little room for doubt over much of the field, is not wholly unequivocal. Some uncertainties remain. We have already referred to them and more will be said presently.

Experience certainly shows convincingly that restrictive practices are generally harmful to growth and efficiency, and it is reasonable to place on those who employ such practices the onus of proving that the public interest would be promoted (or at least not harmed) by their continuance. This policy is in conformity with the proposition that some kind of competitive pressure (workable competition) is the most effective way of encouraging efficiency and enterprise, and is dispensed with at peril. The anti-trust policy of the Americans has been derived directly from the principle that competition is socially beneficial, and the British, after a period of coy uncertainty, have moved much nearer than formerly to the same standpoint by their legislation of 1956 and 1964. Indeed, by the Resale Prices Act, they have carried the application of the principle even further than the American legislators in one sphere, the retail trade.

Competition may be introduced into some markets simply by the abolition of existing restrictive practices and by ensuring that these are not replaced by devices with the same effect. Elsewhere, however, positive steps to foster it may be necessary, as by opening up new sources of supply, or breaking down market imperfections. We have observed that these methods, as well as devices for strengthening centres of countervailing power, have been employed in the service of British anti-monopoly policy. Up to this point the problem is fairly straightforward. It is when monopolies of scale are encountered that the major difficulties arise. No doubt if the authorities apply the principle that all actions which tend to create or strengthen monopoly are contrary to the public interest, the path to judgment is clear. Even so, the Americans, who have used this magnificently unambiguous principle as a guide, have been confronted with some intricate practical problems when dealing with monopolies of scale. Some of these have arisen from the presence of oligopoly, now characteristic of many modern industries. It is recognized that while oligopolists in some trades may seek, by overt or tacit collusion, to avoid competition, in other trades they may be in fierce rivalry. In other words, a particular structure may be compatible with very different types of business behaviour.

If these complications exist when an attempt is made to apply the principle of workable competition, they are much exaggerated if the criterion of effective business performance is brought in. Both the British and the Continental Europeans are well disposed towards that criterion when reaching judgments about monopolies of scale. To them there are 'good' and 'bad' monopolies just as there are acceptable and unacceptable means of attaining a dominant position in an industry. The difficulties and ambiguities of British policy in such cases are demonstrated by the fact that at a time when the Monopolies Commission has sent forward recommendations (accepted by the Government) to forbid certain proposed mergers, the Government, through the Industrial Reorganization Corporation, has been encouraging consolidations in several British industries, with the object of improving their efficiency and their capacity to meet great foreign rivals on equal terms. Although one may doubt whether these results are *always* to be attained by consolidation, there is nothing logically inconsistent in the policies. Some mergers may be expected to yield beneficial results, others the reverse; but it is often a nice problem in economic judgment to discriminate between them.[1] The EEC, as we have seen, is now facing precisely the same type of problem.

This distinction between 'good' and 'bad' monopolies is one that the Courts in the United States were at one time ready to recognize; the issue then turned on the behaviour of the monopolist. To the British administrators of monopoly policy, who have from the beginning taken account of effective business performance, the distinction has always been admissible. We have observed that in the creation of many great consolidations in the past the twin purposes of improving efficiency and of achieving market dominance, or of increasing countervailing power, have been present. For example, the prospectus issued in 1898 by the Bradford Dyers Association, a combine in the textile finishing trade, gave among the advantages to be obtained by combination both 'the avoidance of loss through undue competition and cutting of prices below cost' and also 'economies due to centralization of office work and of buying, distributing and financial arrangements'.[2] Again, the merger which led to the formation of Imperial Chemical Industries in 1926 was designed 'to promote technical and commercial efficiency and also to make it possible for the British chemical industry to deal with similar large groups in other

[1] The 'code' for mergers promised by the Government is intended to help in solving this problem, but until it appears one must suspend judgment on the usefulness of this device. See p. 129, *supra*.

[2] W. H. B. Court, *British Economic History*, 1870–1914, pp. 254–5.

countries on terms of equality'. It sometimes happens that while a combination aimed at securing dominance in the home market, unaffected by outside competition, would be frowned on, it might well be encouraged if the object were to improve the strategic position of the industry internationally. The combination in January 1968 between British Motor Holdings and Leylands provides an example of a trend in industrial organization which is likely to become more clearly marked as competition in certain branches of the economy takes the form of rivalry in world markets between great national or international concerns. In these circumstances competitive pressure (or workable competition) which, it is widely believed, is essential for keeping firms up to the mark, may be preserved, even though the arena in which it is exerted has become the whole world.

This discussion, however, does not entirely settle the debate on the economic consequences of monopoly itself, for the conclusion reached depends on the presence of competition in some form. We need not reiterate the arguments about the benefits or disadvantages of monopoly as such, the arguments between those who believe that monopoly is likely to produce the inertia associated with established authority and those who, like Schumpeter and Galbraith, consider that only great dominating concerns can command the resources needed for most types of industrial innovation, or the security essential for large-scale investment in new plant. It may well be that this conflict of opinion on monopoly cannot be resolved on the plane of broad generalized statements at all. It is possible that no conclusion which is generally applicable can be reached and that the consequences of monopoly for technical progress may differ greatly from one type of society or economic environment to another.

In a country in which a high proportion of the most able men follow a business career, in which incomes are rising fast and capital accumulation proceeding rapidly, the appearance of monopoly in certain sectors of the economy may give rise to few deleterious consequences. In such a society it is not merely easier for entirely new enterprise to find adequate scope, but there, also, even large established businesses are alert in seizing opportunities for entering on lines of trade which have hitherto been the province of other firms. 'The gale of creative destruction' that blows through the society destroys the risk of monopolistic stagnation. The great firm has not merely the means to be progressive; in that environment it cannot survive unless it has the will to be progressive.

The appearance of monopoly in some sectors of industry may have very different consequences for a poorer and less fluid society where the flow of new savings is small, and where the rapid enlargement of incomes, though desired, is subordinated as an end of policy to the preservation of status. There, monopoly once established in any industry may be difficult to disturb, either by the incursion of new firms or by the encroachment of one great firm on the province of others. In such a society, within which the disposition of established authority towards inertia finds a congenial environment, monopoly may constitute a powerful means of reinforcing an existing tendency towards technical stagnation. It may succeed in repressing innovators who, in its absence, would have been able to launch new ventures. Economists who live in countries of this sort may have valid reasons for being more sceptical of the virtues of monopoly than their American counterparts.

The contention that conclusions about the relation of monopoly to technical progress possess only a local validity may be supported by a further argument. In an underdeveloped country that is intent upon industrializing itself quickly but is dependent upon the outside world for advanced technical knowledge, a high concentration of economic power may be required to stimulate a rapid process of capital formation and to mobilize effectively the scarce resources of expertise and entrepreneurial skill. The modern economic history of Japan furnishes an example of rapid industrial development which took place in circumstances of the extreme concentration of resources and initiative in the hands of a very few great, rival concerns. After the Second World War Japan's industrial recovery and the development of her science-based industries depended initially on the import of technique from the United States. This import was made possible by a series of technical agreements between Japanese and American firms and by joint ventures. In this process the giant business-houses played an essential part. It is doubtful whether a structure composed only of numerous small or medium-sized firms would have attracted the co-operation of foreign enterprise and capital to the same extent. In India, and in several other countries in early stages of industrialization, concentration of control which sometimes amounts to monopoly can be observed. It may be suggested, therefore, that the effect of this type of monopoly on technical and commercial progress is likely to vary from one kind of economic society and economic purpose to another. If this is so, then it seems that we must content ourselves with conclusions that have only a local and temporary relevance.

From principles we may now pass to methods of application. Whether a judicial or an administrative process, or some combination of the two, is chosen, is purely a matter of expediency. Doubts have been expressed, especially by economists, about whether the law courts are satisfactory places for the interpretation and analysis of evidence concerning the economic effects of monopolistic practices and structures, especially as few judges have been trained in economics. From this point of view the procedure followed by the Monopolies Commission in this country is preferable. If it had been possible to modify that procedure so as to remove the businessmen's objections to it, there would have been strong arguments against the change of method introduced by the Restrictive Trade Practices Act. However, to Ministers and civil servants the procedure chosen in 1956 possessed the substantial advantage of transferring the responsibility for irksome decisions in particular cases from the Government to the judiciary. The judges have the duty of interpreting the law without regard to the influence exerted by the groups or concerns affected by their decisions. The long delays and timid compromises that attended the implementation by the Board of Trade of the Commission's recommendations provide a striking example of a government's disposition to shirk its responsibilities when faced by strong sectional interests. So the Court has been more effective than the Commission not because the judicial procedure provides a more reliable or speedier method than the administrative procedure for assessing the economic effects of restrictive practices, but simply because the judges take decisions, whereas the Monopolies Commission can merely offer recommendations to those whose instinct in these matters is to procrastinate.

It is true that some of the judgments of the Restrictive Practices Court look very odd when exposed to economic analysis. Nevertheless, the Court has done much towards eliminating the more noxious restrictive practices and has exerted a salutary influence on business behaviour. So there can be no question of returning to the previous procedure so far as restrictive practices are concerned. But this still leaves ample scope for the Monopolies Commission in scrutinizing monopolies of scale and mergers as well as in discharging the other and lesser responsibilities mentioned on page 116. Unless Great Britain is to become uncharacteristically doctrinaire in its treatment of business organization and to hold that monopoly by its very existence is contrary to the public interest, then one cannot avoid the examination of particular cases 'on their merits' (that is to say, by reference to what a body of experienced and disinterested men judge to be the public interest). It may be that certain practices of single-firm monopolies, in addition to those covered by existing law, can be proscribed with advantage to the public interest. But the advance must be cautious. One of the most obvious candidates for proscription is the policy of price discrimination. Yet, as already indicated, the use of such pricing methods is sometimes justified not only in the case of public utilities (where it may be the only satisfactory way of covering total costs) but also for private manufacturing industry. *Ad hoc* inquiries may distinguish between policies of price discrimination which are consonant with, and those which are hostile to, the public interest, but, as the Americans have found, it is difficult to handle such distinctions by judicial processes.

There is, therefore, room in the United Kingdom for both types of procedure, and further advances in the policy are feasible in both directions.[1] Various proposals have been put forward for strengthening the attack in restrictive practices and for closing the gaps in existing arrangements. Many of these gaps have resulted from the efforts of the associations and their lawyers to find unregistrable substitutes for the arrangements covered by the Restrictive Trade Practices Act. If it were possible to provide that such substitute arrangements should not be entered into without the approval of the Court, one of the chief means of frustrating the intention of the Act would have been removed. A strong body of opinion supports the proposal that 'information' agreements, which in some trades have proved to be effective substitutes for formal restrictive agreements, should be registered.[2] At the same

[1] The Prices and Incomes Board, established in 1965, seems inclined from time to time to encroach on the functions properly reserved to the Monopolies Commission and the Restrictive Practices Court, both in its judgments about proposed price increases in particular industries, and also in its recommendations about market behaviour. For instance, in its report on Road Haulage Rates (in June 1965) it advised the abandonment of the practice by which the Road Haulage Association gives recommendations to its members about changes in rates; this practice, it stated, was against the interests of both the industry and its customers. Again, in the report on Soap and Detergents (in October 1965) the Board condemned the practice by which the producers recommend prices to the retailers and it suggested that the producers should 'embark . . . on more competitive price policies'. The Board's reports on Aluminium Semi-Manufactures, Bricks and the Clearing Banks all contained recommendations about market behaviour and about remedies for unsatisfactory performance. If responsibility for monopoly policy should become more widely diffused, this might give rise to difficulties in administration, and Parliament might have to define more clearly than at present the respective functions of the Board, the Commission, and the Court.

[2] The view of 'information' agreements as merely devices for evading the provisions of the Restrictive Trade Practices Act has been challenged. The dissemination throughout a trade of information about every firm's

time it would be desirable to determine definitely the legal position of the bilateral arrangements by which associations sometimes replace multi-lateral arrangements condemned by the Court, and to make such arrangements registrable. The powers of the Registrar and the Court to deal with failures to register restrictive agreements and with breaches of undertakings by the parties should also be strengthened. At present the Registrar lacks the resources required for searching out unregistered restrictive agreements, and he does not usually discover them until complaints about them have been made. This loophole in the law has led to delays. It should be closed by increasing the Registrar's powers and resources or, preferably, by making the operation of agreements illegal until they have been registered.

It has been suggested that restrictive arrangements of the kind covered already by the Restrictive Trade Practices Act should be prohibited without making any provision for exceptions; that is to say, that the 'gateways' should be abolished. Such an amendment to the existing law would certainly save time and effort. To judge from the cases so far decided by the Court any harm done by so summary a treatment would probably be far more than offset by its advantages. It is unlikely, however, that so drastic a proposal would command agreement sufficient to persuade Parliament to

---

prices, output and intentions should, like all means of reducing ignorance of market conditions, increase the perfection of the market in cases where the firms (or some of them) are intent upon competing with each other. But 'information' agreements in practice are normally drawn up with the object of restricting competition. Whether the effect is then harmful to the public interest or not depends, so it is argued, on circumstances. Thus, the increase of knowledge about each other, while it may restrain short-run price competition among the firms, may help to ensure that their long-run development policies are soundly based. On the other hand, the effect may be simply that of discouraging all forms of competition. In face of these complications, doubt has been expressed about whether the law can distinguish between 'information' agreements that are likely to be damaging to the public interest and those that may be beneficial to it. Reference of these cases to the Monopolies Commission may be preferable to the adoption of a judicial procedure. See G. B. Richardson, 'Price Notification Schemes', *Oxford Economic Papers*, November 1967.

legislate accordingly. It is not sufficient to show that on balance this course would be the most expeditious and satisfactory. As long as there is some reason for believing that in exceptional cases cartels may possess advantages for a substantial section of the community (as, for example, the 'depression' cartels which are tolerated in some countries for industries in a state of temporary depression or of chronic decline), then Parliament is not likely to deny some opportunity for claiming exemption from the general prohibition, although it may well see reason for narrowing the 'gateways'.

Debate on this question illustrates the difficulties of the legal procedure in the control of monopoly. There is sound sense in Adam Smith's famous dictum: 'People of the same trade seldom meet together, even for merriment and diversion, but the conversation ends in a conspiracy against the public, or in some contrivance to raise prices.' But it must be qualified. One should distinguish between the arrangements among traders that are detrimental to the public interest and the co-operation among them that is constructive and conducive to enhanced efficiency. Joint action to solve common problems, either in the technical or in the commercial field, may be highly advantageous both to the trade and to the public, and it would be foolish to frustrate co-operative efforts likely to have that effect. But in this, as in loftier matters, it is difficult for a legal rule 'to keep the mean between two extremes, of too much stiffness in refusing and too much easiness in admitting variations from it'.[1]

Another proposal, which has been provoked by a recognition of the defects of the judicial procedure, is that associations on the

[1] Agreements which may offend under the Restrictive Trade Practices Act may sometimes be viewed with favour by government departments or government agencies concerned with promoting particular industrial policies. Such agreements, for instance, may include co-operative arrangements about standardization, investment policy, research or even prices. No doubt, room must be left for some flexibility in the administration of policy on restrictive practices. But it is not easy to see how this problem can be completely resolved, for some of these inconsistencies rest upon a fundamental conflict of principle.

Register of Restrictive Practices should be required to send in a report on each year's working to the Board of Trade. This report would provide figures of production, profit and investment for all their members. The Board of Trade would scrutinize each report, and if it found what appeared to be an unsatisfactory performance, it would then refer the cartel to a Commission of Enquiry.[1] The Commission after investigation might declare the agreement void. This proposal is probably impracticable, if only because it would impose a vast load of work on the Board of Trade, which is ill equipped to deal with it. Moreover, the long delay which the procedure would entail before decisions were reached might well keep in existence many restrictive agreements which under the present law do not long survive.

Some critics of the Monopolies Commission have claimed that it should have undertaken, for each of its references, detailed investigations into productive and commercial efficiency and should have included in its reports recommendations based on the results. This is to misjudge the Commission's purpose. It is not, and should not be, constituted to act as management consultants. If it is to be effective, its functions must be limited. When certain practices or policies pursued by a monopolist have been deemed detrimental to efficiency, the Commission has drawn attention to them. But it is one thing to try to estimate the effects of particular trade practices or policies and quite another to pass judgment on the efficiency of an organization as a whole to which many diverse factors make their contribution. On the other hand, there is much to be said in favour of the Monopolies Commission's having power to advise on the selection of references, for this might help to avoid wasting time on trivialities and to concentrate effort on the economically significant rather than on the politically expedient. The recent extension of the Commission's scope to cover services is to be welcomed. But there is no reason to stop at that point. Many problems encountered in the public sector are identical with those

[1] For details of this proposal, see C. Brock, *The Control of Restrictive Practices from* 1956, pp. 141–3.

in the private sector, and the Commission is as suitable as any other body for investigating and reporting on them. The price policies of nationalized undertakings might well be brought under its scrutiny, and the same is true of several of the marketing and pricing arrangements found in agriculture, such as those administered by the Milk Marketing Board. All these suggestions, however, still leave unremarked the most essential condition of a satisfactory anti-monopoly policy, namely the will of the Government to prosecute it effectively. The criticisms directed from time to time at the Monopolies Commission for its slowness and ineffectiveness should properly have been levelled at the Government which has often shown indifference and timidity in dealing with the Commission's recommendations.

In future the threats to the policy's success may be of another kind. When towards the end of the Second World War the monopoly policy was first adumbrated, most of the politicians, civil servants and industrialists held it to be of minor importance among the economic issues of the new era. There is now a tendency in some quarters to regard the monopoly policy as a panacea for all our industrial ills. The truth is that while it can help to promote enterprise and to mould an environment in which innovating talent flourishes, it cannot of itself create these qualities nor supply all the deficiencies of a stagnating industrial system. The avoidance of exaggerated claims and hopes is thus essential if the policy in the end is not to be discredited. Similarly, the reputation of the bodies concerned with carrying out the policy will depend in some degree on their good sense in recognizing the limits on their capacity to prescribe remedies. Where the line is to be drawn is, of course, debatable, and there is ample room for disagreement in particular cases. Fortunately, the recommendations of the Commission and the decisions of the Court are exposed to informed criticism, and errors in judgment are not likely to escape censure.

Finally, critics of the administrative and judicial machinery set up in the United Kingdom to deal with monopoly and restrictive practices should not overlook, in a vain search for an ideal world, the real benefits that have been gained, and are likely to be gained in future, from the pursuit of the policy examined in this book. It is true that, so far, the activities of the Monopolies Commission and the Restrictive Practices Court have not made British industry as a whole vigorously competitive, nor outstandingly more efficient than in the past. But they have at least succeeded in some degree during the last twenty years in changing the attitude of British businessmen towards competition and monopoly; they have certainly helped to 'loosen up' a formerly very rigid industrial structure; and they have done something towards enabling the enterprising to make their way in markets once tightly controlled. This can be considered a reasonable achievement, even though it may not satisfy political idealists innocent of industrial or administrative experience.

Appendix A

THE MONOPOLIES AND RESTRICTIVE PRACTICES (INQUIRY AND CONTROL) ACT, 1948

(i) EXTRACT FROM *Section 3*

Conditions to which Act applies

3.—(1) Conditions to which this Act applies shall be deemed for the purposes of this Act to prevail as respects the supply of goods of any description if either—

(*a*) at least one-third of all the goods of that description which are supplied in the United Kingdom or any substantial part thereof are supplied by or to any one person, or by or to any two or more persons, being interconnected bodies corporate, or by or to any such two or more persons as are described in subsection (2) of this section; or

(*b*) any agreements or arrangements (whether legally enforceable or not) are in operation the result of which is that, in the United Kingdom or any substantial part thereof, goods of that description are not supplied at all.

(2) The two or more persons referred to in subsection (1) of this section are any two or more persons who, whether voluntarily or not, and whether by agreement or arrangement or not, so conduct their respective affairs as in any way to prevent or restrict competition in connection with the production or supply of goods of the description in question (whether or not they themselves are affected by the competition and whether the competition is between persons interested as suppliers or producers or between persons interested as customers of suppliers or producers):

Provided that in considering whether or not any two or more persons so conduct their affairs as aforesaid, practices as to the workers to be employed or not to be employed by them or as to the remuneration, conditions of employment, hours of work or working conditions of workers, or any class of workers, so employed shall be left out of account.

(*Section 4* makes the same provision in respect of the application of any process to goods.)

(ii) *Section 14*: THE PUBLIC INTEREST

14. In determining whether any conditions to which this Act applies or any things which are done by the parties concerned as a result of, or for the purpose of preserving, any conditions to which this Act applies, operate or may be expected to operate against the public interest, all matters which appear in the particular circumstances to be relevant shall be taken into account and, amongst other things, regard shall be had to the need, consistently with the general position of the United Kingdom, to achieve—

(*a*) the production, treatment and distribution by the most efficient and economical means of goods of such types and qualities, in such volume and at such prices as will best meet the requirements of home and overseas markets;

(*b*) the organization of industry and trade in such a way that their efficiency is progressively increased and new enterprise is encouraged;

(*c*) the fullest use and best distribution of men, materials and industrial capacity in the United Kingdom; and

(*d*) the development of technical improvements and the expansion of existing markets and the opening up of new markets.

Appendix B

THE RESTRICTIVE TRADE PRACTICES ACT, 1956

(i) *Section 6*: Registration of Agreements

6.—(1) Subject to the provisions of the two next following sections, this Part of this Act applies to any agreement between two or more persons carrying on business within the United Kingdom in the production or supply of goods, or in the application to goods of any process of manufacture, whether with or without other parties, being an agreement under which restrictions are accepted by two or more parties in respect of the following matters, that is to say—

(*a*) the prices to be charged, quoted or paid for goods supplied, offered or acquired, or for the application of any process of manufacture to goods;

(*b*) the terms or conditions on or subject to which goods are to be supplied or acquired or any such process is to be applied to goods;

(*c*) the quantities or descriptions of goods to be produced, supplied or acquired;

(*d*) the processes of manufacture to be applied to any goods, or the quantities or descriptions of goods to which any such process is to be applied; or

(*e*) the persons or classes of persons to, for or from whom, or the areas or places in or from which, goods are to be supplied or acquired, or any such process applied.

(2) For the purposes of the foregoing subsection it is immaterial whether any restrictions accepted by parties to an agreement relate to the same or different matters specified in that subsection, or have the same or different effect in relation to any matter so specified, and whether the parties accepting any restrictions carry on the same class or different classes of business.

(3) In this Part of this Act 'agreement' includes any agreement or arrangement, whether or not it is or is intended to be enforceable (apart from any provision of this Act) by legal proceedings, and references in

this Part of this Act to restrictions accepted under an agreement shall be construed accordingly; and 'restriction' includes any negative obligation, whether express or implied and whether absolute or not.

(4) For the purposes of this Part of this Act an agreement which confers privileges or benefits only upon such parties as comply with conditions as to any such matters as are described in paragraphs (*a*) to (*e*) of subsection (1) of this section, or imposes obligations upon parties who do not comply with such conditions, shall be treated as an agreement under which restrictions are accepted by each of the parties in respect of those matters.

(5) Without prejudice to the last foregoing subsection, an obligation on the part of any party to an agreement to make payments calculated by reference—

(*a*) to the quantity of goods produced or supplied by him, or to which any process of manufacture is applied by him; or

(*b*) to the quantity of materials acquired or used by him for the purpose of or in the production of any goods or the application of any such process to goods, being payments calculated, or calculated at an increased rate, in respect of quantities of goods or materials exceeding any quantity specified in or ascertained in accordance with the agreement, shall be treated for the purpose of this Part of this Act as a restriction in respect of the quantities of those goods to be produced or supplied, or to which that process is to be applied.

(6) This Part of this Act shall apply in relation to any agreement made by a trade association as if the agreement were made between all persons who are members of the association or are represented thereon by such members and, where any restriction is accepted thereunder on the part of the association, as if the like restriction were accepted by each of those persons.

(7) Where specific recommendations (whether express or implied) are made by or on behalf of a trade association to its members or to any class of its members, as to the action to be taken or not taken by them in relation to any particular class of goods or process of manufacture in respect of any matter described in the said subsection (1), this Part of this Act shall apply in relation to the agreement for the constitution of the association notwithstanding any provision to the contrary therein, as if it contained a term by which each such member, and any person repre-

sented on the association by any such member, agreed to comply with those recommendations and any subsequent recommendations made to them by or on behalf of the association as to the action to be taken by them in relation to the same class of goods or process of manufacture and in respect of the same matter.

(8) In this section 'trade association' means a body of persons (whether incorporated or not) which is formed for the purpose of furthering the trade interests of its members, or of persons represented by its members; and for the purposes of this section, two or more persons being inter-connected bodies corporate or individuals carrying on business in partnership with each other shall be treated as a single person.

(ii) *Section 21*: Presumption as to the Public Interest

21.—(1) For the purposes of any proceedings before the Court under the last foregoing section, a restriction accepted in pursuance of any agreement shall be deemed to be contrary to the public interest unless the Court is satisfied of any one or more of the following circumstances, that is to say—

(*a*) that the restriction is reasonably necessary, having regard to the character of the goods to which it applies, to protect the public against injury (whether to persons or to premises) in connection with the consumption, installation or use of those goods;

(*b*) that the removal of the restriction would deny to the public as purchasers, consumers or users of any goods other specific and substantial benefits or advantages enjoyed or likely to be enjoyed by them as such, whether by virtue of the restriction itself or of any arrangements or operations resulting therefrom;

(*c*) that the restriction is reasonably necessary to counteract measures taken by any one person not party to the agreement with a view to preventing or restricting competition in or in relation to the trade or business in which the persons party thereto are engaged;

(*d*) that the restriction is reasonably necessary to enable the persons party to the agreement to negotiate fair terms for the supply of goods to, or the acquisition of goods from, any one person not party thereto who controls a preponderant part of the trade or business of acquiring or supplying such goods, or for the supply of goods to any person not party to the agreement and not carrying on such a trade or business who, either alone or in combination with any other such person, controls a preponderant part of the market for such goods;

(*e*) that, having regard to the conditions actually obtaining or reasonably foreseen at the time of the application, the removal of the restriction would be likely to have a serious and persistent adverse effect on the general level of unemployment in an area, or in areas taken together, in which a substantial proportion of the trade or industry to which the agreement relates is situated;

(*f*) that, having regard to the conditions actually obtaining or reasonably foreseen at the time of the application, the removal of the restriction would be likely to cause a reduction in the volume or earnings of the export business which is substantial either in relation to the whole export business of the United Kingdom or in relation to the whole business (including export business) of the said trade or industry; or

(*g*) that the restriction is reasonably required for purposes connected with the maintenance of any other restriction accepted by the parties, whether under the same agreement or under any other agreement between them, being a restriction which is found by the Court not to be contrary to the public interest upon grounds other than those specified in this paragraph, or has been so found in previous proceedings before the Court, and is further satisfied (in any such case) that the restriction is not unreasonable having regard to the balance between those circumstances and any detriment to the public or to persons not parties to the agreement (being purchasers, consumers or users of goods produced or sold by such parties, or persons engaged or seeking to become engaged in the trade or business of selling such goods or of producing or selling similar goods) resulting or likely to result from the operation of the restriction.

(2) In this section 'purchasers', 'consumers' and 'users' include persons purchasing, consuming or using for the purpose or in course of trade or business or for public purposes; and references in this section to any one person include references to any two or more persons being inter-connected bodies corporate or individuals carrying on business in partnership with each other.

Appendix C

THE RESALE PRICES ACT, 1964

(i) *Section 1, Subsection (1)*: Avoidance of Conditions for Maintaining Resale Prices

1.—(1) Subject to the provisions of this Act with respect to registration and to the powers of the Restrictive Practices Court thereunder, any term or condition of a contract for the sale of goods by a supplier to a dealer, or of any agreement between a supplier and a dealer relating to such a sale, shall be void in so far as it purports to establish or provide for the establishment of minimum prices to be charged on the resale of the goods in the United Kingdom; and it shall be unlawful for any supplier of goods (or for any association or person acting on behalf of such suppliers)—

(*a*) to include in any contract of sale or agreement relating to the sale of goods any term or condition which is void by virtue of this section;

(*b*) to require, as a condition of supplying goods to a dealer, the inclusion in any contract or agreement of any such term or condition, or the giving of any undertaking to the like effect;

(*c*) to notify to dealers, or otherwise publish on or in relation to any goods, a price stated or calculated to be understood as the minimum price which may be charged on the resale of the goods in the United Kingdom.

(ii) *Section 2*: Prohibition of other Measures for Maintaining Resale Prices

2.—(1) Subject to the provisions of this Act with respect to registration, to the powers of the Restrictive Practices Court thereunder and to the next following section, it shall be unlawful for any supplier to withhold supplies of any goods from a dealer seeking to obtain them for resale in the United Kingdom on the ground that the dealer—

(*a*) has sold in the United Kingdom at a price below the resale price goods obtained, either directly or indirectly, from that supplier, or has supplied such goods, either directly or indirectly, to a third party who had done so; or (*b*) is likely, if the goods are supplied to him, to sell them in the United Kingdom at a price below that price, or supply them, either directly or indirectly, to a third party who would be likely to do so.

(2) In this section 'the resale price', in relation to a sale of any description, means any price notified to the dealer or otherwise published by or on behalf of a supplier of the goods in question (whether lawfully or not) as the price or minimum price which is to be charged on or is recommended as appropriate for a sale of that description, or any price prescribed or purporting to be prescribed for that purpose by any contract or agreement between the dealer and any such supplier.

(3) For the purposes of this Act a supplier of goods shall be treated as withholding supplies of goods from a dealer—

(*a*) if he refuses or fails to supply those goods to the order of the dealer;

(*b*) if he refuses to supply those goods to the dealer except at prices, or on terms or conditions as to credit, discount or other matters, which are significantly less favourable than those at or on which he normally supplies those goods to other dealers carrying on business in similar circumstances; or

(*c*) if, although he contracts to supply the goods to the dealer, he treats him in a manner significantly less favourable than that in which he normally treats other such dealers in respect of times or methods of delivery or other matters arising in the execution of the contract.

(4) For the purposes of this Act a supplier shall not be treated as withholding supplies of goods on any such ground as is mentioned in subsection (1) of this section if, in addition to that ground, he has other grounds which, standing alone, would have led him to withhold those supplies.

(5) In any case where, by virtue of this section, it would be unlawful for a supplier to withhold supplies of goods, it shall also be unlawful for him to cause or procure any other supplier to do so.

(iii) *Section 3*: Exception for Measures Against Loss-leaders

3.—(1) It shall not be unlawful by virtue of section 2 of this Act for a supplier to withhold supplies of any goods from a dealer, or to cause or procure another supplier to do so, if he has reasonable cause to believe that within the previous twelve months the dealer or any other dealer to whom the dealer supplies goods has been using as loss-leaders any goods of the same or a similar description, whether obtained from that supplier or not.

(2) The reference in this section to the use of goods as loss-leaders is a reference to a resale of the goods effected by the dealer, not for the purpose of making a profit on the sale of those goods, but for the purpose of attracting to the establishment at which the goods are sold customers likely to purchase other goods or otherwise for the purpose of advertising the business of the dealer:

Provided that a sale of goods shall not be treated for the purposes of this section as the use of those goods as loss-leaders—

(*a*) where the goods are sold by the dealer at a genuine seasonal or clearance sale, not having been acquired by the dealer for the purpose of being resold as mentioned in this section; or

(*b*) where the goods are resold as mentioned in this section with the consent of the manufacturer of the goods or, in the case of goods made to the design of a supplier or to the order and bearing the trade mark of a supplier, of that supplier.

(iv) *Section 5, Subsection (2)*: Exemption of Particular Classes of Foods

(2) An order under this section directing that goods of any class shall be exempted goods may be made by the Restrictive Practices Court if it appears to the Court that in default of a system of maintained minimum resale prices applicable to those goods—

(*a*) the quality of the goods available for sale, or the varieties of the goods so available, would be substantially reduced to the detriment of the public as consumers or users of those goods; or

(*b*) the number of establishments in which the goods are sold by retail would be substantially reduced to the detriment of the public as such consumers or users; or (*c*) the prices at which the goods are sold by retail would in general and in the long run be increased to the detriment of the public as such consumers or users; or

(*d*) the goods would be sold by retail under conditions likely to cause danger to health in consequence of their misuse by the public as such consumers or users; or

(*e*) any necessary services actually provided in connection with or after the sale of the goods by retail would cease to be so provided or would be substantially reduced to the detriment of the public as such consumers or users,

and in any such case that the resulting detriment to the public as consumers or users of the goods in question would outweigh any detriment to them as such consumers or users (whether by the restriction of competition or otherwise) resulting from the maintenance of minimum resale prices in respect of the goods.

Appendix D

THE MONOPOLIES AND MERGERS ACT, 1965

(i) *Section 3, Subsections (4), (5) and (6)*: POWERS OF BOARD OF TRADE IN RELATION TO MONOPOLY SITUATIONS

(4) The Board may—

(*a*) declare it to be unlawful, except to such extent and in such circumstances as may be provided by or under the order—

(i) to discriminate in any manner specified or described in the order between any persons in the prices charged for goods or services so specified or described, or to do anything so specified or described which appears to the Board to amount to such discrimination, or to procure others to do any of the things above mentioned;

(ii) to give or agree to give in other ways any such preference as respects the supply of goods or services, or the giving of orders for goods or services, as may be so specified or described, or to do anything so specified or described which appears to the Board to amount to giving such a preference, or to procure others to do any of the things above mentioned;

(iii) to charge for goods or services supplied prices different from those in any published list or notification, or to do anything so specified or described which appears to the Board to amount to charging such prices;

(*b*) require a person supplying goods or services to publish a list of or otherwise notify prices, with or without such further information as may be so specified or described;

(*c*) regulate to such extent and in such circumstances as may be provided by or under the order the prices to be charged for any goods or services so specified or described,

but the Board shall not, in relation to goods or services of any class to which the report relates, exercise the power conferred by virtue of paragraph (*c*) above unless it appears to the Board on the facts found by the Commission as stated in the report that prices charged in the case of goods or services of that class are, or have been, such as to operate, or to be expected to operate, against the public interest.

(5) The Board may prohibit or restrict the acquisition by any person of the whole or part of the undertaking or assets of another person's trade or business, or the doing of anything which will or may result in any bodies corporate becoming interconnected bodies corporate, or may require that, if such an acquisition is made or anything is done which has that result, the persons concerned or any of them shall thereafter observe any prohibitions or restrictions imposed by or under the order.

(6) The Board may provide for the division of any trade or business by the sale of any part of the undertaking or assets or otherwise (for which purpose all the activities carried on by way of trade or business by any one person or by any two or more interconnected bodies corporate may be treated as a single trade or business), or for the division of any group of interconnected bodies corporate, and for all such matters as may be necessary to effect or take account of the division, including—

(*a*) the transfer or vesting of property, rights, liabilities or obligations;

(*b*) the adjustment of contracts, whether by the discharge or reduction of any liability obligation or otherwise;

(*c*) the creation, allotment, surrender or cancellation of any shares, stock or securities;

(*d*) the formation or winding-up of a company or other association, corporate or unincorporated, or the amendment of the memorandum and articles or other instruments regulating any company or association;

(*e*) the extent to which, and the circumstances in which, provisions of the order affecting a company or association in its share capital, constitution or other matters may be altered by the company or association, and the registration under any enactment (including an enactment of the Parliament of Northern Ireland) of the order by companies or associations so affected;

(*f*) the continuation with any necessary change of parties of any legal proceedings.

(ii) *Section 6, Subsections (1) and (2)*: New Powers in Relation to Mergers

6.—(1) Where it appears to the Board of Trade that it is or may be the fact that—

(*a*) two or more enterprises, one at least carried on in the United

Kingdom or by or under the control of a body corporate incorporated in the United Kingdom, have, not earlier than six months previously, ceased to be distinct enterprises; and

(*b*) either—

(i) as a result, the following conditions prevail, or do so to a greater extent, as respects the supply of goods or services of any description, that is to say, as respects the supply of goods of any description, at least one-third of the goods of that description which are supplied in the United Kingdom or any substantial part thereof are supplied by or to any one person, or by or to the persons by whom the enterprises (so far as they continue to be carried on) are carried on, or, as respects the supply of services of any description, the supply of services of that description in the United Kingdom or any substantial part thereof is, to the extent of at least one-third, by or for any one person, or by or for the persons by whom the enterprises so far as they continue to be carried on) are carried on; or

(ii) the value of the assets taken over exceeds five million pounds;

the Board of Trade may, if they think fit, refer the matter to the Commission for investigation and report and, if they do so, shall publish the reference in such manner as they think most suitable for bringing it to the notice of the persons affected:

Provided that paragraph (*b*)(i) above shall not apply where the prevalence of the conditions in question is expressly authorized by or under any enactment, other than the enactments relating to patents and trade marks.

(2) On a reference under this section the Commission shall investigate and report on the facts, that is to say (subject to subsection (4) below) on the question whether subsection (1)(*a*) and (*b*) above are satisfied; and if the Commission find they are satisfied, the Commission shall also investigate and report whether the fact of the enterprises having ceased, in the circumstances of the case, to be distinct enterprises operates or may be expected to operate against the public interest; and if the Commission so find, the Commission shall consider whether any and if so what action (whether under this Act or otherwise and whether by a Minister of the Crown, Government department or other authority or by the parties concerned themselves) should be taken to remedy or prevent any mischiefs which result or may be expected to result, and may, if they think fit, include recommendations as to such action in their report.

Select Bibliography

BOOKS

BAIN, J. S., *Industrial Organization*. London, 1959

BROCK, C., *The Control of Restrictive Practices from* 1956. London, 1966

CHAMBERLIN, E. H., (Ed.), *Monopoly and Competition and their Regulation*. London, 1954

DEWEY, D., *Monopoly in Economics and Law*. Chicago, 1959

EDWARDS, C. D., (Ed.), *Proceedings of the International Conference on the Control of Restrictive Business Practices*. Chicago, 1960

EVELY, R., and LITTLE, I. M. D., *Concentration in British Industry*. London, 1960

GALBRAITH, J. K., *American Capitalism*. London, 1952

GUENAULT, P. H., and JACKSON, J. M., *The Control of Monopoly in the United Kingdom*. London, 1960

HUNTER, A., *Competition and the Law*. London, 1966

MASON, E. S., *Economic Concentration and the Monopoly Problem*. Cambridge, Mass., 1957

MCLACHLAN, D. L., and SWANN, D., *Competition Policy in the European Community*. London, 1967

MILLER, J. P., (Ed.), *Competition, Cartels and their Regulation*. London, 1962

NEALE, A. D., *The Anti-trust Laws of the United States of America*. London, 1960

PICKERING, J. F., *Resale Price Maintenance in Practice*. London, 1966

RICHARDSON, G. B., *Information and Investment*. London, 1960

ROBINSON, E. A. G., *Monopoly*. London, 1941

ROWLEY, C. K., *The British Monopolies Commission*. London, 1966

SCHUMPETER, J. A., *Capitalism, Socialism and Democracy*, London, 1942

STEVENS, R. B., and YAMEY, B. S., *The Restrictive Practices Court*. London, 1965

STOCKING, G. W., and WATKINS, M. W., *Monopoly and Free Enterprise*. New York, 1951

SUMMERFIELD, H., and STANBROOK, I., *The Resale Prices Act*. London, 1964

THORELLI, H. B., *The Federal Anti-trust Policy*. London, 1954

YAMEY, B. S., *The Economics of Resale Price Maintenance*. London, 1951

ARTICLES AND PAMPHLETS

ARMSTRONG, A., and SILBERSTON, A., 'Size of Plant, Size of Enterprise and Concentration in British Manufacturing Industry, 1935–58', *Journal of the Royal Statistical Society*, Series A, Vol. 128, Part 3, 1965

BEACHAM, A., 'Some Thoughts on the Cement Judgment', *Economic Journal*, June 1962

CLAY, H., 'The Campaign against Monopoly and Restrictive Practices', *Lloyds Bank Review*, April 1952

DENNISON, S. R., 'The Restrictive Trade Practices Court in Action', *Yorkshire Bulletin of Economic and Social Research*, December 1959

GEORGE, K. D., 'Changes in British Industrial Concentration, 1951–58', *Journal of Industrial Economics*. July 1967

HEATH, J. B., 'Restrictive Practices Legislation; Some Economic Consequences', *Economic Journal*. September 1960; 'The Restrictive Practices Court on Competition and Price Restriction', *Manchester School*. January 1960

HEFLEBOWER, R. B., 'Recent American Anti-trust Experience', *Three Banks Review*. June, 1960

JEWKES, J., 'Monopoly and Economic Progress', *Economica*. August 1953

MCLACHLAN, D. L., and SWANN, D., 'Competition Policy in the Common Market', *Economic Journal*. March 1963; '*Concentration or Competition; a European Dilemma*' (Chatham House). London, 1967

O'BRIEN, D. P., and SWANN, D., 'Information Agreements: a Problem in Search of a Policy', *Manchester School*. September 1966

PICKERING, J. F., 'The Enforcement of Resale Price Maintenance, 1956–64', *Public Law*. Autumn 1966

PLANT, A., 'Economic Theory Concerning Patents for Inventions', *Economica*. 1934

RICHARDSON, G. B., 'Price Notification Schemes', *Oxford Economic Papers*. November 1967

SUTHERLAND, A., 'Economics in the Restrictive Practices Court', *Oxford Economic Papers*. November 1965; 'Are Books Different?;, *The Solicitor Quarterly*. October 1963

WISEMAN, J., 'Monopoly, Technical Progress and Public Policy', *Yorkshire Bulletin of Economic and Social Research*. June 1956

WISEMAN, J., LLOYD, A., and HEATH, J. B., 'Symposium on Restrictive Practices Legislation', *Economic Journal*. September 1960

YAMEY, B. S., 'Water Tube Boilers', *Modern Law Review*. January 1960; 'Restrictive Agreements and the Public Interest', *Public Law*. Summer 1960; 'The Monopolies Commission Report on Cigarettes and Tobacco', *Modern Law Review*. November 1961; 'Some Issues in our Monopoly Regulations', *Three Banks Review*. June 1962; *Resale Price Maintenance* (Hobart Paper). 1964

OFFICIAL PUBLICATIONS

Monopolies and Restrictive Practices (Enquiry and Control) Act, 1948
Monopolies and Restrictive Practices Commission Act, 1953
Restrictive Trade Practices Act, 1956
Resale Prices Act, 1964
Monopolies and Mergers Act, 1965
Board of Trade, *Report of Committee on Resale Price Maintenance*, 1949; *Annual Reports on the Operation of the Monopoly and Restrictive Practices Act*
Monopolies (and Restrictive Practices) Commission, *Reports*
Registrar of Restrictive Trading Agreements, *Reports* (Cmnd. 1273), 1961; (Cmnd. 1603) 1962; (Cmnd. 2246) 1964
White Paper on *Monopolies, Mergers and Restrictive Practices* (Cmnd. 2299). March 1964
United States Senate Sub-Committee on Trust and Anti-trust, *Reports:* on *Administered Prices* (1957); and on *Economic Concentration* (1965)
Commission of the EEC, *Practical Guide to Articles* 85 *and* 86 *of the Treaty of Rome and Implementing Regulations* (Translation in Board of Trade Journal, October 19, 1962); *General Reports on the Activities of the Community*. Annual
British Iron and Steel Federation, *Translation of Treaty Establishing The European Coal and Steel Community*. 1951

Index

For Product Safety Concerns and Information please contact our EU representative GPSR@taylorandfrancis.com
Taylor & Francis Verlag GmbH, Kaufingerstraße 24, 80331 München, Germany

www.ingramcontent.com/pod-product-compliance
Lightning Source LLC
LaVergne TN
LVHW011134300926
849160LV00008B/640
9780415607339